D0046096

Craig Evans is the Payzant Distinguished Professor of New Testament at Acadia University and Acadia Divinity College in Nova Scotia, Canada. He has published more than fifty books, many on Jesus and the Gospels, including (with N. T. Wright) *Jesus, The Final Days* (2009). Professor Evans has lectured in many universities and museums around the world and has appeared several times as an expert commentator in television documentaries and news programmes. He is married and has two grown daughters and a grandson.

JESUS AND HIS WORLD

The Archaeological Evidence

CRAIG A. EVANS

WESTMINSTER
JOHN KNOX PRESS
LOUISVILLE • KENTUCKY

First published in the United States of America in 2012 by
Westminster John Knox Press
100 Witherspoon Street
Louisville, KY 40202

First published in Great Britain in 2012 by
Society for Promoting Christian Knowledge
36 Causton Street
London SW1P 4ST

12 13 14 15 16 17 18 19 20 21—10 9 8 7 6 5 4 3 2

Cover design by Dilu Nicholas
Cover Art: © Eldad Carin / istockphoto.com

Library of Congress Cataloging-in-Publication Data

Evans, Craig A.
    Jesus and his world : the archaeological evidence / Craig A. Evans.
        p. cm.
    Includes bibliographical references (p.   ) and indexes.
    ISBN 978-0-664-23413-3 (alk. paper)
    1. Bible. N.T. Gospels—Antiquities. 2. Jesus Christ. I. Title.
    BS621.E885 2012
    2225.9'3—dc23

                                        2011051970

PRINTED IN THE UNITED STATES OF AMERICA

For Master Chief Gator Franklin,
Explosive Ordnance Disposal,
United States Navy,
in appreciation

Contents

Figures

Figures

Preface

The goal of this book is to present what I regard as the most important archaeological discoveries pertaining to Jesus of Nazareth in a way that can be accessed by non-experts. For 20 years now I have myself benefited greatly from visits to active excavations, on-site tours and explanations from archaeologists, their publications and the many fine museums where artefacts are housed, preserved and explained. Among these I especially have in mind the Israel Museum and its Shrine of the Book, the British Museum in London and the Ashmolean Museum in Oxford. I have benefited too from a number of libraries, including Acadia University's Vaughan Memorial Library, Harvard University's Hollis Library, Princeton University's Firestone Library, Princeton Theological Seminary's Speer Library, Yale University's Beinicke Rare Book and Manuscript Library and Oxford University's fabled Bodleian Library, along with the Sackler Library's collection of papyri. To the many patient librarians and accommodating curators I offer my heartfelt thanks.

Among the archaeologists who have been very helpful, providing on-site tours and explanations, are Rami Arav, Gabriel Barkay, Richard Batey, Ronny Reich, James Strange and the late Douglas Edwards. (Acadia was favoured by a visit and several stimulating lectures by Jim Strange and Doug Edwards in the spring of 2008.) I am also grateful to Dirk Obbink for some very helpful show-and-tell in the Sackler papyri room in the autumn of 2009. I also wish to acknowledge the helpful correspondence with Jane Evans, Shimon Gibson, Franck Goddio, Kurt Raveh and Shelly Wachsmann.

I was pleased when the good people at SPCK and Westminster John Knox Press asked me to write this book. I especially thank Rebecca Mulhearn and Philip Law. Part of the book was written during a peaceful stay at the Cistercian Abbaye Notre-Dame du Calvaire in Rogersville, New Brunswick. I extend my thanks to Brother Graham Touchie for the hospitality shown me and for the engaging conversation about Jesus and archaeology. I thank Jeremiah Johnston, PhD (cand.), for assistance in the preparation of the indexes and for carefully reading the manuscript and asking good questions.

The book is dedicated to Master Chief Gator Franklin, Explosive Ordnance Disposal, United States Navy (retired). For 30 years Gator risked life and limb in the excavation, recovery and dismantling of explosives and in training others at home and abroad to do the same. Because of his work countless lives have been saved.

C. A. Evans
Acadia Divinity College

Abbreviations

1 Apol.	Justin Martyr, *First Apology*
1 Clem.	*1 Clement*
AASOR	Annual of the American Schools of Oriental Research
ABD	*Anchor Bible Dictionary*
'Abot	Mishnah: *'Abot*
ABRL	Anchor Bible Reference Library
Ag. Ap.	Josephus, *Against Apion*
Ant.	Josephus, *Jewish Antiquities*
Apol.	Plato, *Apology of Socrates*
b. Ketub.	Babylonian Talmud: *Ketubbot*
b. Meg.	Babylonian Talmud: *Megillah*
b. Mo'ed Qat.	Babylonian Talmud: *Mo'ed Qatan*
b. Pesah.	Babylonian Talmud: *Pesahim*
b. Qidd.	Babylonian Talmud: *Qiddushin*
b. Šabb.	Babylonian Talmud: *Shabbat*
BA	*Biblical Archaeologist*
BAR	*Biblical Archaeology Review*
Bib	*Biblica*
BibOr	Biblica et orientalia
BibSem	Biblical Seminar
CBQ	*Catholic Biblical Quarterly*
CD	Cairo Genizah copy of the *Damascus Document*
CIJ	*Corpus inscriptionum judaicarum*
CIL	*Corpus inscriptionum latinarum*
CIS	*Corpus inscriptionum semiticarum*
CJO	*Catalogue of Jewish Ossuaries* (ed. L. Y. Rahmani)
CJZ	*Corpus Jüdischer Zeugnisse aus der Cyrenaika* (ed. G. Lüderitz)
CRINT	Compendia rerum iudaicarum ad Novum Testamentum
Dial.	Justin Martyr, *Dialogue with Trypho*
Dreams	Philo, *On Dreams*
DSD	*Dead Sea Discoveries*

Embassy	Philo, *On the Embassy to Gaius*
Esth. Rab.	Esther Rabbah
Exod. Rab.	Exodus Rabbah
Haer.	Irenaeus, *Against Heresies*
Hist. eccl.	Eusebius, *Ecclesiastical History*
IEJ	*Israel Exploration Journal*
IG	*Inscriptiones graecae.* Editio minor. Berlin, 1924–
Ign. *Eph.*	Ignatius, *To the Ephesians*
Ign. *Smyrn.*	Ignatius, *To the Smyrnaeans*
Joseph	Philo, *On the Life of Joseph*
JBL	*Journal of Biblical Literature*
JJS	*Journal of Jewish Studies*
JQR	*Jewish Quarterly Review*
JR	*Journal of Religion*
JRASup	Journal of Roman Archaeology: Supplement series
JSHJ	*Journal for the Study of the Historical Jesus*
JSJSup	Journal for the Study of Judaism in the Persian, Hellenistic, and Roman Periods: Supplement Series
JSOT	*Journal for the Study of the Old Testament*
JSPSup	Journal for the Study of the Pseudepigrapha: Supplement Series
J.W.	Josephus, *Jewish Wars*
LÄ	*Lexikon der Ägyptologie*
Lev. Rab.	*Leviticus Rabbah*
Life	Josephus, *The Life*
m. Keritot	Mishnah: *Keritot*
m. Maʿaś. Š.	Mishnah: *Maʿaser Sheni*
m. Meg.	Mishnah: *Megillah*
m. Moʿed Qat.	Mishnah: *Moʿed Qatan*
m. Ned.	Mishnah: *Nedarim*
m. Negaʾim	Mishnah: *Negaʾim*
m. Parah	Mishnah: *Parah*
m. Pesah.	Mishnah: *Pesahim*
m. Šabb.	Mishnah: *Shabbat*
m. Sanh.	Mishnah: *Sanhedrin*
m. Taʿanit	Mishnah: *Taʿanit*
m. Yoma	Mishnah: *Yoma*
Mas	Masada ostraca

MdB	*Le Monde de la Bible*
Moses	Philo, *On the Life of Moses*
Nat.	Pliny the Elder, *Natural History*
NEAEHL	*The New Encyclopedia of Archaeological Excavations in the Holy Land* (ed. E. Stern)
NovT	*Novum Testamentum*
NovTSup	Novum Testamentum Supplements
NTS	*New Testament Studies*
NTTS	New Testament Tools and Studies
OGIS	*Orientis graeci inscriptiones selectae* (edited by W. Dittenberger)
PEQ	*Palestine Exploration Quarterly*
P. Oxy.	Papyri Oxyrhynchus
Ps.-Diogenes	A writing falsely attributed to Diogenes the Cynic
Qoh. Rab.	*Qohelet Rabbah*
RAr	*Revue Archéologique*
RB	*Revue biblique*
REJ	*Revue des études juives*
SBLRBS	Society of Biblical Literature Resources for Biblical Study
SBLSBS	Society of Biblical Literature Sources for Biblical Study
SEG	*Supplementum epigraphicum graecum*
Sipre Deut.	*Sipre Deuteronomy*
Sipre Num.	*Sipre Numbers*
SNTSMS	Society for New Testament Studies Monograph Series
Song Rab.	*Song of Songs Rabbah*
Spec. Laws	Philo, *On the Special Laws*
t. Meʿila	Tosefta: *Meʿila*
t. Menah.	Tosefta: *Menahot*
T. Mos.	*Testament of Moses*
t. Qidd.	Tosefta: *Qiddushin*
t. Šabb.	Tosefta: *Shabbat*
t. Sukkah	Tosefta: *Sukkah*
Tg. Ps.-J.	*Targum Pseudo-Jonathan*
TSAJ	Texte und Studien zum antiken Judentum

WUNT	Wissenschaftliche Untersuchungen zum Neuen Testament
y. Ketub.	Jerusalem Talmud: *Ketubbot*
y. Meg.	Jerusalem Talmud: *Megillah*
y. Moʿed Qat.	Jerusalem Talmud: *Moʿed Qatan*
ZNW	*Zeitschrift für die neutestamentliche Wissenschaft und die Kunde der älteren Kirche*

Introduction

In a column that appeared in a popular archaeology magazine, respected Professor of Hebrew Bible Ron Hendel provides a succinct definition of biblical archaeology: 'Biblical archaeology,' says Hendel, 'involves the rigorous correlation of textual data from the Bible and material evidence from archaeology.'[1] Quite so. If archaeologists and historians could not find correlation between archaeology and the biblical text, there would be no such thing as 'biblical archaeology'. But of course they do find such correlation, and lots of it. This is why there are many magazines and journals devoted to archaeology, a great many scholarly reference works on archaeology and countless scholarly and popular books that treat this subject from every conceivable angle.

What archaeologists and historians find can also be called verisimilitude, or 'resemblance to the truth'; that is, resemblance or likeness to the way things really were. This means that the writings of the Bible speak of real people, real places and real events. Many of these things can be corroborated by archaeological discoveries and by other ancient sources. Often what archaeologists uncover is not so much *proof* but *clarification*.[2] The Bible may talk about a given people, a particular place or a major event, but little detail is provided. The precise meaning of the text is unclear. Then an archaeological discovery is made and we understand the story much better.

Of course, archaeology sometimes does prove things. For instance, let's consider what is called biblical minimalism, which is usually in reference to the Old Testament or Hebrew Bible. Here I have in mind especially those minimalists who have argued that David and Solomon are fictional characters, that there was no kingdom of Israel reaching back to the tenth century BCE and that if they existed, there was not the level of literacy required to record the chronicles of such persons and their deeds. Some of these minimalists think the narratives of the Hebrew Bible do not date any earlier than the fifth century BCE. As it turns out – thanks to archaeology – the minimalists are wrong on all these points.

In 1993 and 1994, fragments of a ninth-century BCE stone inscription, incised by the king of Syria, were found at Tel Dan (today's northern Israel) during excavations conducted by Avraham Biran, a respected Israeli archaeologist. The first inscription found contains the words, 'the house of David'. Most agree that it is very unlikely that an inscription of this nature would be incised only a century or so after the supposed existence of a legendary, unhistorical personage. Would a Syrian king speak of a mythical 'House of David' as if it were a real, enemy dynasty? Unlikely. It seems David really did exist after all.[3]

The minimalists retreated but did not give up. Maybe there was a David. But was he a *king*, the head of a centralized government with far-flung territories, or was he little more than a local tribal chieftain? Not surprisingly, the minimalists argued for the latter. Strange when you think of it, given the implications of the geographical location of the Tel Dan Inscription (that is, far north of Judea and Jerusalem, near the disputed boundary between Syria and Israel). In any case, the minimalists have again been proven wrong.

Archaeological excavations in the oldest part of Jerusalem have uncovered significant evidence of a centralized, organized government complex. Artefacts have been dated to the tenth century BCE, the era of David and his son Solomon. Radio carbon dating at Megiddo, Qeiyafa and elsewhere has confirmed the emergence of an Iron Age kingdom of David some time around 1000 BCE, very much as the biblical narratives relate. Not quite ready to surrender, some minimalists suggested that Qeiyafa was Philistine instead of Israelite. But alas, archaeological excavations uncovered no pig or dog bones at Qeiyafa (in contrast to Gath, a Philistine city, where non-kosher animals were eaten), but excavations at Qeiyafa did reveal building architecture consistent with what is typically found in Judea (but not in Philistine cities).[4]

And finally, the famous ostracon (an inscribed potsherd) recently found at Qeiyafa, which dates to the tenth century, offers dramatic proof of the level of literacy required to record the history of the kings of Judah and Israel. The find does not prove that portions of the books of Samuel and Kings date this far back, but it does show that records could have been produced – and, if other related discoveries are anything to go on, would have been produced – on which the authors of Samuel and Kings would have drawn.[5] I am not sure if the biblical minimalists will ever run up the white flag, but I think most agree that they have indeed fallen on hard times.[6]

I briefly mention the setbacks suffered by Old Testament minimalists because they illustrate the danger of asserting the non-existence of this or the lack of historicity of that simply on the grounds that we only possess an ancient story. We must remember that only 5 per cent of the sites of the biblical world have been excavated; and most of these sites have only been partially excavated. In any case, must every ancient narrative be corroborated by archaeological discoveries? If we insisted on archaeological corroboration before trusting our literary sources, very little history – biblical or otherwise – could be written.

New Testament minimalists have suffered similar setbacks, especially with reference to Jesus and the Gospels. At one time it was fashionable to assert that the early Christian confession of Messiah Jesus as 'Son of God' arose not from Jewish and Old Testament antecedents (2 Sam. 7.14; Ps. 2.2, 7, for example) but from the influence of the Greco-Roman world, where Greek kings and Roman emperors were hailed as sons of the gods. The discovery of 4Q246, comprising two columns of Aramaic text from Qumran's fourth cave, demolished this view. The author of this first-century BCE text anticipated the coming of a deliverer who will be called 'Son of God' and 'Son of the Most High'. The remarkable parallels to the language of the annunciation (Luke 1.31–35) are widely acknowledged. It seems that Aramaic-speaking Jews at least one generation before the time of Jesus hoped for a messiah who would be described in rather exalted terms. Post-Easter competition with the Roman imperial cult was not required for the followers of Jesus to speak of their risen Master as the Son of God.

For much of the twentieth century a number of New Testament scholars assumed that Jesus possessed no messianic consciousness; that recognition of him as Messiah was a post-Easter development. The publication of 4Q521 put that negative conclusion to rest. A fragment of this Qumran scroll anticipates the appearance of God's Messiah, whom heaven and earth will obey. When this Messiah comes the downtrodden will be raised up, the injured will be healed, the dead will be raised up and the poor will hear good news. Scholars immediately recognized the parallels with Jesus' reply to the imprisoned John the Baptist: 'Go and tell John what you hear and see:

the blind receive their sight and the lame walk, lepers are cleansed and the deaf hear, and the dead are raised up, and the poor have good news preached to them' (Matt. 11.4–5; Luke 7.22). The authenticity of the passage is doubted by almost no one; and now its messianic import is widely recognized. Did Jesus understand himself as God's anointed, as the Messiah? It seems he did.[7]

Other minimalists have suggested that there were no synagogue buildings in the time of Jesus; that the New Testament Gospels, which refer to these buildings, are anachronistic. As we shall see, archaeological discoveries have demolished this position. Others have suggested that Galilean Jews were not especially Torah-observant but had embraced a great deal of Greek culture and thought. In such an imagined world Jesus might have been more of a Hellenistic Cynic than a Jewish teacher or prophet. Archaeology has again set the record straight. It has also been suggested that the body of Jesus might not have been taken down from the cross and placed in a tomb. Perhaps the Gospels' accounts of his burial are nothing more than fiction and apologetic. Then again, perhaps Jesus was buried and we have found his tomb, including his ossuary and the ossuaries of his wife and son. Jesus was not resurrected but he did have a family! And on it goes. Yet in every case, as we shall see, archaeology, sometimes assisted by related and corroborating documents, has shown how baseless these novel theories really are.

The award for the all-time minimalist theory goes to Canadian author Tom Harpur, whose book *The Pagan Christ* garnered a lot of attention a few years ago. Harpur is convinced that Jesus of Nazareth is only a mythical figure, not a person of history.[8] In New Testament studies this is the ultimate minimalist position! After all, it is one thing to say that tenth-century BCE King David might not have existed, but to say that first-century CE Jesus of Nazareth didn't exist is quite another matter.

In an interview published recently in the *United Church Observer*, the lapsed Christian had this to say in response to scholars – conservative and liberal alike – who 'take the historical Jesus pretty seriously':

Yeah, but they don't offer a shred of historical evidence. Since my book was published, there has not been one scholar come forth with solid evidence from the first century, apart for (*sic*) a dubious reference in Josephus that they love to hurl around, a reference that is clearly, clearly, clearly false. I've been waiting for the evidence to show up.[9]

What Harpur asserts in this paragraph is quite astonishing. Is his claim true? Is there really no evidence, not even a 'shred' of evidence, that Jesus lived?

Harpur is not alone. Another lapsed Christian and former clergy-man, Robert Price, has also expressed serious doubts, though at times he seems open to the possibility that a man named Jesus once lived. In any case, Price believes the evidence for the existence of Jesus is at best very, very thin. Like Harpur, Price rejects almost every argument or proffered piece of evidence that there was a Jesus of history.

Not surprisingly, the radical scepticism of Harpur and Price has gained no scholarly following. Harpur's strange theory, in which he resurrects the theosophic views and pseudo-Egyptology of Gerald Massey and Alvin Boyd Kuhn among others, has been thoroughly refuted and is not followed by any reputable historian or Egyptologist.[10] No major historian or New Testament scholar follows Price either.[11] The views of Harpur and Price are of no interest – if even known – to the members of the Society of New Testament Studies, an elite inter-national group of scholars who serve on the faculties of the finest universities around the world. Even the much larger and inclusive Society of Biblical Literature offers no programme units centred on the theme of the non-existence of Jesus or Jesus as a mythological embodiment of an Egyptian religious concept. The views of Harpur and Price are seen as quite eccentric. Nevertheless, their radical scepti-cism provides us with opportunity in this brief Introduction to review the evidence for Jesus, which will provide a clearer context for the present book.

What is the evidence for Jesus? Do we have, in the words of Tom Harpur, 'solid evidence from the first century'? Yes, we do. We have four narrative accounts, which in time came to be called Gospels. Of these four, three – Matthew, Mark and Luke – were written in the first century, in the 60s and 70s. Some will argue for earlier dates; others will argue for later. No competent historian or New Testament scholar argues for a second-century date of these Gospels. Most scholars agree that the Gospel of John was published before the end of the first century. Even if we set aside John because of its lateness and its obvious metaphorical portrait of Jesus, we have in Matthew, Mark and Luke, known as the Synoptic Gospels, three accounts written at the end of the first generation of the Jesus movement, when some eyewitnesses were still living. One of them explicitly refers to 'those who from the beginning were eyewitnesses' (Luke 1.2). Most historians of late antiquity would be thrilled to have three complete accounts of a historical figure written within one generation of the time that figure lived.

We also have the testimony of Paul (d. *c*.65), who after a year or two of persecuting the Jesus movement was converted and became a believer and member of it. Paul wrote a number of letters – just how many is disputed – from the late 40s to the early 60s. In these letters, especially 1 Corinthians and Galatians, he mentions some of Jesus' original disciples as well as James, the brother of Jesus. He calls them 'pillars' of the church and discusses his not always cordial relations with them. In one place Paul says he 'went up to Jerusalem to visit Cephas, and remained with him fifteen days' (Gal. 1.18). The rsv, which I have quoted, translates 'to visit'. But the underlying word *historēsai* – from which we get our word 'history' – means 'to inquire of' or 'get information from'. Paul did not simply go to Jerusalem to visit Peter (Aramaic: Cephas), the premier disciple of Jesus; he went to Jerusalem 'to get information from Peter'.[12]

That Paul did in fact learn at least some of the Jesus story from those who had known him during his public ministry is seen in a number of references in the apostle's letters. Ten times Paul mentions the cross; that is, the cross on which Jesus suffered death by crucifixion. In poetic praise Paul says Jesus 'humbled himself and became obedient unto death, even death on a cross' (Phil. 2.8). Ten times Paul uses the verb crucify/crucified. Almost every occurrence is a reference to the crucifixion of Jesus: 'We preach Christ crucified' (1 Cor. 1.23); 'Jesus Christ and him crucified' (1 Cor. 2.2); 'he was crucified in weakness' (2 Cor. 13.4). Dozens of times Paul speaks of the death of Jesus: 'who was put to death for our trespasses' (Rom. 4.25); 'Christ died for the ungodly' (Rom. 5.6); 'the death of his Son' (Rom. 5.10); 'the death he died he died to sin' (Rom. 6.10). Paul also repeats the words Jesus spoke during his final meal with his disciples (1 Cor. 11.23–25).

In reminding the Christians of Corinth of the importance of the resurrection, Paul rehearses the tradition that he had 'received', namely 'that Christ died for our sins in accordance with the scriptures, that he was buried, that he was raised on the third day in accordance with the scriptures' (1 Cor. 15.3–4). He goes on to recount the resurrection appearances to Cephas (Peter), the twelve, 'more than five hundred brethren at one time' (most of whom were still living at the time of writing 1 Corinthians), to James, to 'all the apostles' and finally to Paul himself (vv. 5–8). There is little doubt Paul is speaking of a real person, a historical person, a person who had lived, who had died and who had been raised up and seen by a number of people, including those who had known him before his death.

Before leaving first-century documents and eyewitnesses, the testimony of a few others, born in the first century and acquainted either with original disciples or with those who knew them, should be mentioned. I begin with Papias (*c*.60–130 CE). We are told that this man was a disciple of the apostle John – or perhaps another, otherwise unknown, John – and a companion of Polycarp (Irenaeus, *Haer.* 5.33.4). During his childhood the Gospels were written and began to circulate. In the latter part of his life Papias served as bishop of Hierapolis in Asia Minor (Eusebius, *Hist. eccl.* 3.39.13). He is known for his five-volume work, *The Oracles of the Lord*, which only survives in quotations in the writings of Irenaeus the apologist (*c*.130–200) and Eusebius the historian (*c*.260–340). At the beginning of this lost work Papias explains that he never passed up the opportunity to seek information from 'elders' who in earlier years had been personally acquainted with the apostles (and here Papias names Andrew, Peter, Philip, Thomas, James, John and Matthew). From the elders who had been acquainted with the original followers of Jesus, Papias learned that Mark, assistant to the apostle Peter, wrote the Gospel of Mark and that the apostle Matthew composed the oracles of Jesus 'in the Hebrew dialect' (Eusebius, *Hist. Eccl.* 3.39).[13]

We have one quotation of the work of the apologist Quadratus (*c*.70–130): 'But the works of our Saviour were always present, for they were true; those who were healed and those who rose from the dead were seen not only when they were healed and when they were raised, but were constantly present, and not only while the Saviour was living, but even after he had gone they were alive for a long time, so that some of them survived to our own time' (in Eusebius, *Hist. eccl.* 4.3.1–2). In his defence of the Christian faith, Quadratus claims not only that eyewitnesses of the ministry of Jesus were still living in 'our own time' – that is, at the end of the first century – but that so too were some of those who had been healed by him.[14]

Others could be mentioned. Polycarp (*c.*69–156), we are told, was 'the companion of the apostles, who had been appointed bishop of the church of Smyrna by the eyewitnesses and ministers of the Lord' (Eusebius, *Hist. eccl.* 3.36.1). As noted above, he was also a companion of Papias. Other early leaders in the church, whose writings have survived, may be mentioned. Among these is Clement of Rome (flourished in the 90s), who oversaw the letter (*1 Clement*) that was written and sent to the Christians in Corinth (*c.*96). The author of this letter alludes to several sayings of Jesus but apparently not the Gospels themselves (for example *1 Clem.* 13.1–2). It is suspected that Clement has drawn upon early, pre-Synoptic materials. In any case, there is no doubt that for Clement and the people to whom he writes, Jesus was a historical figure, not a symbol or myth: 'The apostles received the gospel for us from the Lord Jesus Christ; Jesus the Christ was sent forth from God. So then Christ is from God, and the apostles are from Christ. Both, therefore, came of the will of God in good order' (*1 Clem.* 42.1–2). Ignatius (*c.*35–*c.*110), bishop of Antioch, wrote a number of letters to churches in Asia Minor, including one to Polycarp. His letters, all written in the last year of his life, contain allusions to the teaching of Jesus. Ignatius may have had access to the Gospel of Matthew (for example Ign. *Eph.* 14.2; Ign. *Smyrn.* 1.1) and perhaps also the Gospel of Luke (for example Ign. *Smyrn.* 3.2).[15]

In short, we have a significant number of people who knew Jesus and who knew those who knew Jesus. We have an unbroken chain of transmission from the time of Jesus himself on through the first century and on into the second and third centuries and beyond. We have writings from people who knew Jesus (one or two of the Gospels, perhaps also the letters of James, Jude and 1 Peter) and from people acquainted with the original family members and disciples of Jesus (such as Paul, probably Papias and perhaps also Clement, Ignatius and Polycarp). The suggestion that all of these people were mistaken in supposing that Jesus was a real person, when in fact he was not, is absurd and flies in the face of common sense.

If we are guided by the criteria by which recognized historians are guided, then we may conclude that there is indeed, contra Harpur, 'solid evidence from the first century'. There is no need to appeal to the disputed passage in Josephus (*Ant.* 18.63–64; cf. 20.200–201), though its cavalier dismissal by Harpur, as well as by Price, is uncritical and unjustified. A number of careful, respected scholars have concluded that this passage, minus a few obvious interpolations, is authentic, demonstrating that Josephus (37–c.100 CE) was well aware that Jesus was the founder of the Christian movement and that he had been condemned by the ruling priests and crucified by the Roman governor Pontius Pilate. The testimony of Josephus is in fact very important, even if it is not crucial.[16]

There is also a very important argument in favour of the general reliability of the New Testament Gospels, and that concerns what is called verisimilitude; that is, what the Gospels describe matches the way things really were in early first-century Jewish Palestine.[17] The New Testament Gospels and Acts exhibit a great deal of verisimilitude. They speak of real people (such as Pontius Pilate, Herod Antipas, Annas, Caiaphas, Herod Agrippa I and II, Felix and Festus) and real events (deaths of John the Baptist and Agrippa I). They speak of real places (villages, cities, roads, lakes and mountains) that are clarified and corroborated by other historical sources and by archaeology. They speak of real customs (Passover, purity, sabbath, divorce law), institutions (synagogue, temple), offices/officers (priests, tax collectors, Roman governors, Roman centurions) and beliefs (of Pharisees and Sadducees; interpretation of Scripture). Jesus' engagement with his contemporaries, both supporters and opponents, reflects an understanding of Scripture and theology that we now know, thanks to the Dead Sea Scrolls and related literature, to have been current in pre-70 Jewish Palestine.

The verisimilitude of the New Testament Gospels stands in contrast to the lack of verisimilitude in the second-century Gospels and Gospel-like writings, such as the *Gospel of Thomas*, the *Gospel of Peter* and the various Gnostic Gospels. It is such that historians and archaeologists of all stripes regularly make use of them, as perusal of their books reveals.[18] These scholars see them as valuable sources, without which historical and archaeological work concerned with first-century Jewish Palestine would be much more difficult. No archaeologist or historian would say this with regard to *Thomas* or *Peter*. It is to the New Testament Gospels that archaeologists and historians make reference.

If the New Testament Gospels were nothing more than fictions and fables about a man who never lived, one must wonder how it is they possess so much verisimilitude and why they talk so much about people we know lived and about so many things we know happened. After all, the Gospels say Jesus was condemned to the cross by a Roman governor named Pontius Pilate. Not only is this man mentioned by historical sources outside the New Testament but we have found an inscribed stone on which his name appears. Indeed, we may have found the name of the Jewish high priest who condemned Jesus inscribed on a bone box. It seems these people were real – I suspect Jesus was too!

The present book stands in this tradition. It is not written to prove that Jesus really lived or that he really was Jewish after all. It's not a book written for internet sceptics, whose pseudo-criticism is not guided by the norms of genuine research and scholarship. Rather it is written for those who want to know what light contemporary archaeology sheds on Jesus and his world; who want to know what aspects of Jesus' teaching and activities we have come to understand better thanks to archaeological discoveries.

In the chapters that follow I treat five major topics. Chapter 1 examines the archaeological findings at Sepphoris, a city only a few kilometres from Nazareth, the village in which Jesus grew up. These findings say a lot about the Galilee of the time of Jesus. They also challenge a novel theory proposed some years ago that suggested that Jesus was a Cynic and not too Jewish in outlook. The proposal raises the question, 'Just how Jewish was Jesus?' Chapter 2 assesses the archaeological and inscriptional evidence for the existence of synagogue buildings in the time of Jesus. Did they really exist, as the Gospels say? If they did, what was their function? These questions are important, for the Gospels suggest that the synagogue was a major component of the setting of Jesus' teaching, preaching and healing.

Chapter 3 explores further the world of Jesus and his contemporaries by inquiring into the evidence of literacy and book culture in the early first century. Who could read, and what did they read? The Gospels portray a literate Jesus who sometimes engaged literate opponents. Does archaeology support this portrait? Chapter 4 looks at what light archaeology sheds on those whom Jesus engaged, sometimes very critically; that is, the ruling priests and Roman authorities. To understand better what happened to Jesus in Jerusalem it is important to know more about the powerbrokers of his day.

Chapter 5 looks at Jewish burial traditions and what archaeology has told us. These traditions tell us a lot about the death and burial of Jesus, as we should assume. But they also tell us a lot about his teaching and ministry and why large crowds were attracted to him. I have also included an Appendix (Appendix 1) that will, among other things, pursue a related topic a bit further. Here I have in mind the remarkable claim made by a Canadian television journalist who said that he had found the tomb of Jesus – with trace remains of Jesus, his wife and his son! Could this be true, and if not, why not?

Before bringing this introduction to a close, a few words need to be said about what archaeology is and how terribly scientific and technical it can be. Archaeology is concerned with the recovery of material culture. In this book this means the material culture of first-century Israel. Material culture includes buildings, roads, sculpture (and other forms of artistic expression), tools, clothing, footwear, ceramics, coins, jewellery, inscriptions (including graffiti), books and other writings and human remains. Archaeology partners with a number of disciplines, including geography, topography, anthropology, history, sociology, botany and other physical sciences. In recent years the subdiscipline of marine archaeology has made great progress and a number of exciting discoveries.

Archaeology and the related disciplines just mentioned are greatly aided by modern technology. These include Neutron Activation Analysis, whereby we can trace pottery, wherever it is found, to its source. This has been hugely significant in our understanding of how seriously the Jewish people took their laws and customs of food purity. Another important technology is Digital Imaging Enhancement, whereby we can 'see' text no longer visible to the naked eye. DNA analysis of parchment and vellum aids scholars in piecing together, identifying and segregating scrolls and bookrolls that survive as scattered fragments. Radiocarbon dating, or Accelerator Mass Spectrometry (AMS), as it is now known, helps us date otherwise undated materials. These include manuscripts, clothing, wood and other materials that at one time were living.

Thanks to modern technologies we can see what is *below*, we can see *from above* and we can see *within*. How do we see below the surface? Ground Penetrating Sonar helps the archaeologist know where to dig, for this technology identifies patterns and anomalies below the surface. Two technologies are related. The first is Magnetometry, which identifies the magnetic 'signatures' of rock. Closely related is Electrical Resistivity Tomography, which identifies different types of rock beneath the surface. Together these technologies help researchers determine what is in the ground.

How do we see from above? Satellite photography can reveal patterns and anomalies that the earthbound archaeologist might not otherwise notice. Faint outlines of buildings, cities and roads can sometimes be seen from orbit, far above the surface of the planet. What we look for are signs of disturbance or alteration of the natural lie of the land caused by forces other than nature.

How do we see within? CAT scans and X-rays help researchers see what is 'inside' (of mummies, books, containers, whatever). What we observe is sometimes quite amazing. We can also see more deeply within. Chemical and element analysis assists archaeologists discover the properties and composition of artefacts and things that accompany artefacts (such as how the ink was made or the presence or non-presence of authentic patina).

In the chapters that follow, some of these technologies will come into play. But I will try to keep things at a level the non-expert can follow. There are also endnotes, but not too many. They should assist readers who want to pursue topics in greater detail. Also at the end of the book are some suggestions for further reading. I hope you will enjoy this book and find the discoveries of archaeology and related fields as exciting as I have.

1

In the shadow of Sepphoris: growing up in Nazareth

Jesus grew up in Nazareth of Galilee – of that there is little doubt. He was known as 'Jesus of Nazareth' (Matt. 21.11; Mark 1.24; Luke 18.37; John 1.45; Acts 2.22; also Matt. 4.13; Mark 1.9; Luke 2.39) – not, for example, 'Jesus of Capernaum' or 'Jesus of Bethlehem'. Nazareth was a small village with a population somewhere between 200 and 400. The Synoptic Gospels refer to a synagogue in Nazareth (Matt. 13.54; Mark 6.2; Luke 4.16). There were no pagan temples or schools. In all likelihood not a single non-Jew lived in Nazareth at this time.

Nazareth is located in the Nazareth Mountains in lower Galilee, about 500 metres above sea level. The name 'Nazareth' appears inscribed on a stone tablet that lists the priestly courses (1 Chron. 24.15–16). The second line reads: 'The eighth course [is] Happizzez of Nazareth.' The tablet was found in the ruins of a third- or fourth-century synagogue in Caesarea Maritima.

Recent excavations in and around Nazareth – which today is a city of about 60,000 – suggest that the village in the time of Jesus may not have been a sleepy, isolated place, as many have imagined it. The old, quaint notion that the inhabitants of Nazareth had to look for work in nearby villages and cities is now quite obsolete. The economy of Nazareth was more than sufficiently active to keep her inhabitants fully occupied. There is evidence of vineyards and grape presses, of terrace farming, of olive presses and the manufacture of olive oil and even of stonemasonry. We should also assume the presence of livestock and perhaps also tanning.

The few remains of private dwellings that reach back to first-century Nazareth attest to simple, rustic construction. No public buildings have been found, nor a paved street. There is no evidence of aesthetics or artwork, such as mosaics or frescoes. Private dwellings were made of fieldstones and mud, with roofs supported by poles and overlaid with reeds and mud. These homes were small in size, often subdivided into four small rooms. Sometimes a set of steps alongside an outer wall led to the roof, where lightweight items could be stored or dried in the sun. The story of the men who climb to the roof of the house and then lower their paralysed friend to the spot where Jesus sat teaching (Mark 3.32) provides a vivid example of this kind of private dwelling (Mark 2.1–12). It would not take a large crowd to pack a small house, so that men transporting a sick friend would have no chance to enter the door or even pass through a window. We should imagine many people trying to press forward to hear Jesus, if not to touch him. Those unable to get inside the house would be crowded at the door and struggling to peer through the windows.

The smallness of the private dwellings, along with small windows, is probably presupposed in a saying like this: 'What I tell you in the dark, utter in the light; and what you hear whispered, proclaim upon the housetops' (Matt. 10.27; Luke 12.3). We should imagine Jesus and his disciples seated or reclining in a small house, dimly lit, discussing the rule of God and what it will mean for Israel. Soon, Jesus tells his disciples, the things they now hear spoken quietly in the dark will be shouted from rooftops in the light of day.

The first-century village of Nazareth probably occupied no more than four hectares. Mostly buried beneath a modern city and built over throughout history, Nazareth presents a challenge to archaeologists. Thus far only small portions of the original village have been unearthed. The remains of a first-century house and other remains can be seen in the lowest levels of the Church – or Basilica – of the Annunciation. Whether any of these remains were part of the home of Mary cannot be confirmed, but they do exemplify the modest nature of these simple dwellings.[1]

Nazareth was not isolated from the rest of Galilee. This was another popular myth, still held by some, who speak of Jesus growing up in a place-bound, isolated village.[2] Nazareth is only a few kilometres from Sepphoris, a major city, and is near a main highway that connects Caesarea Maritima (on the Mediterranean) to the southwest to Tiberias (on the Sea of Galilee) to the northwest. Sepphoris, Caesarea Maritima and Tiberias were the three largest and most influential cities in or near Galilee. Jesus grew up near one of them and not far from the highway that linked the other two. How well-travelled these roads were is shown by the pottery evidence. Pottery produced in Kefar Hananya, some 16 kilometres from Sepphoris, has been found everywhere Jews lived in Galilee, and in fact represents some 75 per cent of the pottery used by Jews in Galilee.[3] Because pottery was subject to contamination and therefore had to be replaced frequently, an uninterrupted supply was very important. That one village could serve as the principal supplier in a region the size of Galilee testifies to the network of roads and the active commerce in the time of Jesus. Not too many villages in Galilee were 'isolated' – certainly not one only a few kilometres from Sepphoris.

Although there was probably enough work in Nazareth to keep Joseph and his sons sufficiently occupied, it is possible that they took part in the expansion of nearby Sepphoris during the early years of the administration of Antipas, tetrarch of Galilee (from 4 BCE to 39 CE). Whether or not Jesus ever worked in Sepphoris, the city's close proximity to Nazareth encourages us to assume that he visited the city from time to time.

A visit to nearby Sepphoris

The Jewish reality of Jesus' upbringing and later public ministry is not always properly appreciated in some of the books published in recent years. Most writers, of course, do acknowledge that Jesus was Jewish, but they propose strange contexts and settings in which they think Jesus should be interpreted. Some of these simply did not exist in the Galilee of Jesus' day. One of the most talked-about theories has been the proposal that Jesus was a Cynic. What encouraged this idea was Nazareth's proximity to Sepphoris, which in the time of Jesus exhibited, at least in appearance, Greco-Roman trappings.

In a popular book on the historical Jesus, one scholar argued that Jesus was a 'peasant Jewish Cynic' and that he and his followers were 'hippies in a world of Augustan yuppies'.[4] Although this book is in places quite helpful and sometimes very insightful, most find the Cynic proposal misguided and misleading. Given the notoriety and influence of the book and the fact that at least a few other scholars support the Cynic hypothesis in one form or another, it is necessary to give some attention to it. We shall begin with a review of the most important literary evidence and then take a look at what the archaeology of Sepphoris suggests.

Jesus and the Cynics: the literary evidence

Who were the Cynics (the ancient ones, that is)? What did they believe and how did they live? Cynicism was founded by Diogenes (*c.*412–321 BCE). The nickname 'Cynic' comes from the Greek word *kynikos*, meaning doggish or dog-like. Cynics earned this dubious sobriquet because of their ragged, unkempt appearance. Attractive apparel and grooming meant nothing to them. And – like dogs – Cynics would urinate and defecate, even copulate in public.

The Cynic typically carried a cloak, a beggar's purse, a staff, and usually went barefoot. In a letter to his father, Diogenes says: 'Do not be upset, Father, that I am called a dog and put on a double, coarse cloak, carry a purse over my shoulders, and have a staff in my hand.' It was this dress code of sorts that has encouraged a few scholars to see significant parallels between Jesus and Cynics. After all, so goes the argument, Jesus gave his disciples similar instructions:

> He charged them to take nothing for their journey except a staff; nor bread, no bag, no money in their belts; but to wear sandals and not put on two tunics. (Mark 6.8–9)

> 'Take no gold, nor silver, nor copper in your belts, nor purse for your journey, nor two tunics, nor sandals, nor a staff; for the labourer deserves his food.' (Matt. 10.9–10)

> 'Take nothing for your journey, no staff, nor bag, nor bread, nor money; and do not have two tunics.' (Luke 9.3)

> 'Carry no purse, no bag, no sandals; and salute no one on the road.' (Luke 10.4)

Are Jesus' instructions in step with the Cynic dress code? No – they do not agree with Cynic dress and conduct; in fact they contradict them. The very things Jesus tells his disciples not to take with them – no bag, no tunic – and no staff either, if we follow the version in Matthew and Luke – are the characteristic markers of the true Cynic, as one observer from late antiquity put it: 'What makes a Cynic is his purse and his staff and his big mouth' (Epictetus 3.22.50; see also Lucian, *Peregrinus* 15; Diogenes Laertius, *Lives of Eminent Philosophers* 6.13; Ps.-Diogenes 30.3). There is nothing Cynic in Jesus' instructions to his disciples.

The only parallel with Jesus is simply in giving instructions with regard to what to wear and what to take on one's journey. The only specific agreement is taking the staff (if we follow Mark; if we do not then there is no agreement at all). The staff, however, is hardly distinctive to Cynics. On the contrary: in the Jewish context the staff has a long and distinguished association with the patriarchs, such as Jacob and Judah (Gen. 32.10; 38.18) and the great lawgiver Moses and his brother Aaron (Exod. 4.4; 7.9). Moreover the staff is also a symbol of royal authority, figuring in texts that in later interpretation take on messianic and eschatological significance (for example Gen. 49.10; Isa. 11.4; Ezek. 19.14).

Jesus and the Cynics

We may compare Jesus' instructions to the Cynic instructions.

Jesus to his disciples

Take no gold, nor silver, nor copper in your belts, nor purse for your journey, nor two tunics, nor sandals, nor a staff (Matt. 10.9–10).

Crates to his students

Cynic philosophy is Diogenean, the Cynic is one who toils according to this philosophy, and to be a Cynic is to take a short cut in doing philosophy. Consequently, do not fear the name [Cynic], nor for this reason shun the cloak and purse, which are the weapons of the gods. For they are quickly displayed by those who are honoured for their character (16).

Diogenes to Hicetas

Do not be upset, Father, that I am called a dog [that is 'Cynic'] and put on a double, coarse cloak, carry a purse over my shoulders, and have a staff in my hand (7).

Diogenes to Antipater

I hear that you say I am doing nothing unusual in wearing a double, ragged cloak and carrying a purse (15).

> ### *Diogenes to Anaxilaus*
>
> For a sceptre I have my staff and for a mantle the double, ragged cloak, and by way of exchange, my leather purse is a shield (19).
>
> The full texts of these letters, and on which these translations are based, are in A. J. Malherbe, *The Cynic Epistles* (SBLSBS 12; Missoula, MT: Scholars Press, 1977). Numerical references are Malherbe's.

Besides the question of dress, some scholars suggest that Jesus' worldview is Cynic. Instead of being caught up with materialism and vanity, the Cynic lives a life of simplicity and integrity before God. According to one ancient writer, the 'end and aim of the Cynic philosophy . . . is happiness, but happiness that consists in living according to nature' (Julian, *Orations* 6.193D). Living according to nature also means treating fellow human beings as equals. A few scholars apparently think that is more or less what Jesus taught. Was it? Here are teachings that are sometimes cited to make this point:

'And why are you anxious about clothing? Consider the lilies of the field, how they grow; they neither toil nor spin; yet I tell you, even Solomon in all his glory was not arrayed like one of these. But if God so clothes the grass of the field, which today is alive and tomorrow is thrown into the oven, will he not much more clothe you, O men of little faith? Therefore do not be anxious, saying, "What shall we eat?" or "What shall we drink?" or "What shall we wear?" For the Gentiles seek all these things; and your heavenly Father knows that you need them all. But seek first his kingdom and his righteousness, and all these things shall be yours as well.'   (Matt. 6.28–33)

'You shall love your neighbour as yourself.'   (Mark 12.31; Lev. 19.18)

'For if you forgive people their trespasses, your heavenly Father also will forgive you; but if you do not forgive people their trespasses, neither will your Father forgive your trespasses.'   (Matt. 6.14–15)

Superficially, Jesus' teaching is at points comparable to Cynic teaching. But Jesus' teaching is very different at other, significant points. For one, Jesus did not teach his disciples to pursue happiness and to live according to nature. What he taught was that nature reveals important things about God, namely that he is loving, good and generous. Jesus urges his disciples to have faith and live in the light of God's goodness and care. But in the end the disciple is to seek God's kingdom (or rule) and righteousness. Then all the rest will fall into place. When the core values are understood, the profound differences between Jesus and the Cynics cannot be missed.

And as mentioned already, Cynics were known for flouting social custom and etiquette, such as urinating, defecating and engaging in sexual intercourse in public (Cicero, *De officiis* 1.128; Diogenes Laertius, *Lives of Eminent Philosophers* 6.69; Epictetus, *Discourses* 2.20.10: Cynics 'eat and drink and copulate and defecate and snore'). Cynics could be very coarse and very rude. In fact one was remembered to have retorted: 'What difference does it make to me, from which end the noise comes?' (Seneca, *Moral Epistles* 91.19). There simply is no parallel to this kind of thinking or behaviour in the teaching and lifestyle of Jesus and his disciples.

Jesus did indeed criticize some of his contemporaries for their religiosity, hypocrisy and mean-spiritedness towards the poor and marginalized:

'Thus, when you give alms, sound no trumpet before you, as the hypocrites do in the synagogues and in the streets, that they may be praised by people.' (Matt. 6.2)

'And when you pray, you must not be like the hypocrites; for they love to stand and pray in the synagogues and at the street corners, that they may be seen by people.' (Matt. 6.5)

'And when you fast, do not look dismal, like the hypocrites, for they disfigure their faces that their fasting may be seen by people.' (Matt. 6.16)

'Woe to you, scribes and Pharisees, hypocrites! For you tithe mint and dill and cumin, and have neglected the weightier matters of the law, justice and mercy and faith; these you ought to have done, without neglecting the others.' (Matt. 23.23)

'Woe to you, scribes and Pharisees, hypocrites! For you build the tombs of the prophets and adorn the monuments of the righteous,

saying, "If we had lived in the days of our fathers, we would not
have taken part with them in shedding the blood of the prophets."'
(Matt. 23.29–30)

'You leave the commandment of God, and hold fast the tradition of
people.'
(Mark 7.8)

Admittedly, all of this criticism could well have been uttered by a
Cynic. But this represents only one aspect of Jesus' teaching. Jesus
criticized some of his critics, but he was not crude, nor did he suggest that religious faith was pointless. Herein lies a telling difference
between the worldview of Jesus and the worldview of Cynics. Whereas
the latter railed against religion because the gods, they thought, were
indifferent, Jesus urged his followers to believe in God because he
does take notice and cares deeply. Indeed, some of the utterances
above go on to assure that 'your Father who sees in secret will reward
you' (Matt. 6.6, 18). Accordingly, Jesus urges his disciples to pray,
'for your Father knows what you need before you ask him' (Matt.
6.8). This is not the teaching of the Cynics.

Furthermore, Jesus proclaimed God's rule and urged his disciples
to look to God for deliverance. Jesus longed for the redemption of
his people and believed deeply that the God of Israel would fulfil
the prophecies and promises of old. These hopes and beliefs are not
consistent with Cynic ideology.

Accordingly, I remain completely unpersuaded by the Cynic thesis,
and I am not alone: most scholars concerned with the historical Jesus
also find it very unlikely.[5] This should occasion no surprise, given what
has been said in the last few pages. So why do some scholars compare
Jesus with the Cynics? Good question – let's consider it next.

Jesus and the Cynics: the archaeological evidence

Comparison with Cynic thought was encouraged in part by a number
of parallels, mostly general and mostly reflecting the wisdom and
social criticism of the eastern Mediterranean world of late antiquity.[6] But a major impetus for the exploration of the Cynic model
came, I believe, from archaeological discoveries in the 1970s and
1980s. Boiled down, these discoveries comprise two things related
to our concerns. First, archaeology has shown how widespread the
Greek language was in the time and place of Jesus. Second, it has

shown how urbanized, in Greco-Roman fashion, some parts of Galilee were in the time of Jesus. As it turns out, Galilee was far more integrated into the larger Roman Empire than at one time imagined. Galilee, Samaria and Judea were no backwater.

From these two discoveries some scholars infer the presence of Greco-Roman philosophy in Galilee. The logic goes something like this: where there were Greco-Roman style urban centres, and where Greek was spoken, it follows that there were Greco-Roman philosophers and philosophies; and that means, of course, the presence of Cynics. And then, when Sepphoris, some 6.5 kilometres north of Nazareth, was excavated and found to have possessed a paved main street and several large buildings in Greco-Roman style, it was further concluded that Cynics must have been present in this city as well. And if Cynics were present in Sepphoris, then surely Jewish youths – like Jesus – living in nearby villages like Nazareth would have come under the influence of these itinerant philosophers. This all makes sense, doesn't it? We aren't missing something, are we? Alas, I'm afraid we are indeed missing something – something very important, namely the rest of the evidence.

The impressive discoveries in Galilee in general and in Sepphoris in particular have forced New Testament interpreters to re-evaluate several things. For one, it is no longer tenable to think of Jesus as having grown up in rustic isolation, as was fashionable for so long. No: Jesus grew up in a village within reasonable walking distance from a large urban centre, part of which was perched on top of a hill and would have been visible to the inhabitants of Nazareth. 'A city set on a hill cannot be hid,' as Jesus himself once said (Matt. 5.14).

Furthermore, the great number of Greek inscriptions, as well as Greek literary finds in the Dead Sea region, has led many scholars to conclude that Greek was spoken by many Jews living in Galilee. This does not mean that Greek was their first language – that was Aramaic. But it does mean that Greek was spoken in the time and place of Jesus (and a few scholars think that Jesus himself spoke some Greek).

But the facts that many Jewish Galileans spoke Greek and that there were urban centres in Galilee, such as Sepphoris near Nazareth and Tiberias on the Sea of Galilee just a few kilometres southwest of Capernaum, do not mean that the Jewish people were soft on their historic faith and ready to absorb Greek philosophy, whether Cynicism or something else. Recent Jewish history suggests just the opposite.

One should remember that a century and a half before Jesus was born, the Jewish people, led by the Hasmonean family (Judas Maccabeus and his brothers), fought a bitter war against Antiochus IV and the Greeks in order to preserve Jewish faith and life. Galilean Jews in the time of Jesus were no doubt influenced by Greek thought and customs to some extent, but not to that of embracing ideologies that seriously conflicted with Jewish faith.

And this is just what the archaeological evidence shows: the Jewish faith and lifestyle were taken seriously. So how Jewish or Greek was Sepphoris, the city near the village of Nazareth, in the time of Jesus? This is a very important question. Much of the archaeological work in the 1970s and 1980s revealed the extent of building. Besides paved, colonnaded streets (Figure 1.1) and large buildings, a public

Figure 1.1 Sepphoris street walk
On the right is a mosaic floor and, on the left, a paved, colonnaded street. The colonnaded street reflects Greco-Roman influence.

Figure 1.2 Sepphoris theatre
Although badly weathered, the outline of the lower portion of the
Sepphoris theatre, carved in the bedrock, is readily discernible.

theatre (Figure 1.2) was also excavated. Although it is disputed, it
is likely that the first phase of the theatre was built in the 20s and
that later expansion and renovation took place towards the end
of the century. But it was the further archaeological work in the
1990s, which included the discovery of the city dump, that led to
the conclusion that Sepphoris was a thoroughly Jewish city in the
days of Jesus after all.

Archaeologists are usually able to date the various layers of ancient
cities. One might think of an ancient city as a layered cake – the top
layer is the most recent, the bottom the most ancient. Therefore the
deeper one digs the older the material one finds. For excavations
in Israel dating to the approximate time of Jesus and the early
Church, find the layer that separates the time before from the time
after 70 CE.

Archaeologists and scholars usually assume that most things that existed prior to 70 CE probably have relevance for understanding the world of Jesus, while most things that came into existence thereafter probably do not. Accordingly, it is important to date the remains of Sepphoris that existed prior to 70 CE before drawing conclusions about what this city might tell us about Jesus and his world.

Archaeologists of the land of Israel can usually find the 70 CE layer in the excavation cake because of the devastation that resulted from the Jewish revolt against Rome (66–70 CE). Many cities and villages were badly damaged if not destroyed altogether, and damaged and destroyed buildings often became the fill and foundations on which the new structures were built.

So archaeologists of Sepphoris have found the 70 CE layer, and have found the city dump. The dump is a great find because what is thrown there includes garbage, and garbage reveals a lot about the people who lived at that time, especially when we are interested in knowing if Jews lived in the city and if these Jews lived according to Jewish laws and customs. What archaeologists discovered turned out to be very revealing.

Among the animal remains that date before 70 CE they found no pig bones, which is hard to explain if we are to imagine the presence of a significant non-Jewish population in Sepphoris. In stark contrast to this finding, after 70 CE (that is, after the destruction of Jerusalem by the Roman army and the beginning of rebuilding throughout Israel), and after a sizeable growth in the non-Jewish population, pig bones come to represent 30 per cent of the animal remains. What this suggests is that prior to the Jewish revolt the population of Sepphoris was Jewish and observed Jewish laws and customs. It was only after the revolt that support for Jewish law and practice began to erode. This means that in the time of Jesus – a generation or more before the revolt – there was little and possibly no non-Jewish presence in Sepphoris. And this means no Cynics either.

But there is more evidence that supports this conclusion. Over 100 fragments of stone vessels dating from before 70 CE have been unearthed thus far, again pointing to a Jewish population at Sepphoris concerned with ritual purity (because stone, unlike ceramic vessels, cannot easily be made unclean; see John 2.6). Non-Jews usually didn't bother with expensive, heavy and hard-to-move stone vessels. For them, ceramic vessels for drinking and cooking were quite acceptable. The large number of stone vessels found at Sepphoris is consistent with the absence of pork bones – that is, the people who lived in Sepphoris prior to 70 CE were Jewish and observed Jewish laws and customs. And consistent with concern over personal purity is the presence in Sepphoris of many *miqva'ot* – ritual bathing pools; singular: *miqveh* (see Figure 1.3). Furthermore, a Hebrew pottery fragment and several lamp fragments bearing the image of the menorah – the seven-branched candelabra – have also been found, dating from the early period.

But there is still more. Coins minted at Sepphoris during the pre-70 CE period do not depict the image of the Roman emperor or pagan deities, as was common in the coinage of this time. In contrast,

Figure 1.3 *Miqveh*, Sepphoris
This plastered, stepped immersion pool was uncovered in the basement of a large home at Sepphoris, probably dating to the first century. Many immersion pools have been discovered at Sepphoris, attesting to the Jewish concern with ritual purity.

in the second century CE, long after the Jewish revolt had ended and the population had begun to change, coins were minted at Sepphoris bearing the images of the emperors Trajan (98–117 CE) and Antoninus Pius (138–61 CE), and the deities Tyche and the Capitoline triad (Jupiter, Juno and Minerva). Indeed, in the reign of Antoninus Pius the city adopted the name Diocaesarea, in honour of Zeus (Dio) and the Roman emperor (Caesar).

The contrast in the findings at Sepphoris

Before 70 CE

What was found:	*What was not found:*
immersion pools (*miqva'ot*)	pig bones
menorah	coins with image of Caesar
fragments of stone vessels	pagan idols and images
	pagan buildings

After 70 CE

What was found:
pig bones
coins with image of Caesar
pagan idols and images
mosaics with pagan themes

What has not been found in pre-70 CE Sepphoris is just as important as what has been found. Excavations have not uncovered any structures typically present in a Greco-Roman city, such as pagan temples, gymnasium, odeum, nymphaeum or shrines and statues, all of which were offensive to Jewish sensibilities. One way of looking at it is that devout Jews were not advocates of multi-culturalism. It is only in the post-70 CE period that pagan art and architecture begin to make their appearance, such as the beautiful mosaic in the mansion depicting pagan themes (Figure 1.4).

All this evidence leads to the firm conclusion that Sepphoris in Jesus' day was a thoroughly Jewish city.[7] There is absolutely no reason whatsoever to think there may have been Cynics loitering

Figure 1.4 Sepphoris Mona Lisa
This beautiful floor mosaic graces the *triclinium* ('reclining on three sides') of the dining room of an impressive mansion, dating to the third century. The face of the lady of the manor, dubbed by some the 'Mona Lisa of Galilee', is prominently depicted (lower centre).

in the streets of Sepphoris on the lookout for Jewish youths from nearby Nazareth.

Commitment to the Jewish laws and customs is in fact seen throughout Galilee; it is not limited to Sepphoris. Throughout Galilee the distribution of Jewish and non-Jewish pottery is very suggestive of this conclusion. Whereas non-Jews purchased Jewish pottery, the Jews of Galilee did not purchase and make use of pottery manufactured by non-Jews. The point here is that because non-Jews had no purity issues in the use of ceramic and pottery, they were happy to buy ceramic from any source – Jewish or non-Jewish. But not so in the case of Jews. Because, in their view, ceramic was susceptible to impurity, Jews therefore purchased pottery only from Jews, never from non-Jews. Accordingly, Jewish pottery that dates prior to 70 CE is found in Jewish and non-Jewish sectors in and around Galilee, while non-Jewish pottery is found only in the non-Jewish sectors. These patterns of distribution strongly suggest that the Jewish people of Galilee were scrupulous in their observance of Jewish purity laws.

Given the evidence that Galilee in Jesus' time was populated with a Jewish people committed to their biblical heritage, and given the complete absence of evidence of any kind of Cynic presence in nearby Sepphoris (or anywhere else in Galilee for that matter), the Cynic hypothesis strikes me as completely lacking in foundation. Moreover it is quite unnecessary – much better parallels for Jesus' teaching can be found in the early literature of the Rabbis and the even earlier Dead Sea Scrolls.

Before leaving Sepphoris, something should be said about its theatre. Archaeologists are divided over the question of its date. All agree that it was enlarged some time in the second half of the first century to accommodate an audience of 4,000. The dispute concerns the date of the earliest phase of the theatre, which may have seated about 2,500. Some archaeologists claim that the theatre was built during the city's expansion under Antipas. If a smaller version of the theatre existed in the time of Jesus, we may have a number of allusions to it in Jesus' teaching. One immediately thinks of the mocking references to the 'hypocrites'. The word itself was originally neutral, meaning 'actor' or 'play-actor' (Diodorus Siculus 37.12.1), though by the first century CE, 'hypocrisy' had also come to mean sanctimonious pretence. This is how Jesus used the word in criticizing those who acted out their piety in an ostentatious or insincere manner. But his use of 'hypocrite' in Matthew 6, and perhaps elsewhere, such as in Matthew 23, probably also reflected the presence and function of the theatre in nearby Sepphoris. There are a number of specific parallels with theatre and acting, beyond the word hypocrite itself.[8]

Jesus warns his disciples not to practise their piety 'before people, in order to be seen by them' (Matt. 6.1). To be 'seen' – or 'watched', from *theathenai*, which is from the root that gives us 'theatre' – may envisage a public performance, something done before an audience. This word by itself would not bring to mind the theatre, but Jesus piles up other terms and activities. These include making a show of charitable donations: 'So whenever you give alms, do not sound a trumpet before you, as the hypocrites do' (6.2). In the theatre of late antiquity, trumpets often announced an action or a new scene. There are also traditions about trumpets sounding for prayer or worship – in for example the Cairo Damascus document (CD) 11.21–22; *m. Ta'anit* 2.5 – but no Jewish traditions sounding trumpets in connection with almsgiving. The sounding of the trumpet comes from the Greek theatre, not the Jewish temple or synagogue.

Jesus also instructs, 'When you give alms, do not let your left hand know what your right hand is doing, so that your alms may be done in secret' (6.3–4). Again we may have an allusion to the theatre, in which actors skilfully coordinated the motions of their hands to complement their words and make more vivid in the minds of the audience what they were to imagine. The hands of the actors were supposed to be synchronized and meaningful, drawing attention to what was being said or done (on this, see Marcus Fabian Quintilian, *Institutio Oratoria* (on stage and orations) 11.2.42; 11.3.66; 11.3.70, 85–121; esp. 114: 'The left hand never properly performs a gesture alone, but it frequently acts in agreement with the right'). Against such well-orchestrated and polished performances, Jesus says, 'Do not let your left hand know what your right hand is doing.'

Jesus warns his disciples not to 'be like the hypocrites; for they love to stand and pray in the synagogues and at the street corners, so that they may be seen by others' (Matt. 6.5). Standing and praying in public may once again allude to the performance of the actor (or 'hypocrite'), who in the theatre stands and gives a soliloquy. It has been observed that the word *plateia*, meaning 'street' (one of the words in the translation 'street corners'; literally 'corners of streets', *en tais goniais ton plateion*), was used of the colonnaded street in nearby Sepphoris. The image may be that of a actor standing in a busy thoroughfare speaking loudly, hoping to attract an audience to the theatre.[9]

Finally, when Jesus enjoins his disciples not to 'look dismal' when they fast so that they will not be 'like the hypocrites' who 'disfigure their faces that their fasting may be seen by people' (Matt. 6.16), he once again may be alluding to the actors or street-corner mimes who paint their faces in order to play their part.

The coherence between Jesus' mockery of the religious hypocrites of his day and the actors and theatre of the time, whether at Sepphoris or elsewhere, suggests that Jesus probably shaped his criticisms and sarcasm to reflect the theatre. The archaeological work at nearby Sepphoris may have relevance for understanding better this aspect of Jesus' teaching.

There is no evidence that during his ministry Jesus visited Sepphoris. It has been suggested that he may have alluded to actors and theatrics, which could further suggest that he may have visited the theatre of Sepphoris at an earlier time in his life. But the absence of any mention of a visit to Sepphoris during his public travels and activities is curious. Indeed, there is no evidence that Jesus visited any of the great cities of Galilee and nearby territories, such as Tiberias on the Sea of Galilee and Caesarea Maritima on the Mediterranean Sea. In fact the only major Galilean city he approached was Caesarea Philippi, near the northern border. Yet even in this case we are told that he only went 'to the villages of Caesarea Philippi' (Mark 8.27) or 'into the district of Caesarea Philippi' (Matt. 16.13), not into the city itself. The avoidance of the cities is curious. In Judea, Jesus visited Jericho and Jerusalem but in Galilee he apparently entered no city. If the Gospels do not narrate any visits to Galilean cities, are there hints, nevertheless, that during his Galilean ministry Jesus was familiar with urban centres? There are such hints.

Jesus and the cities

There are indications in his teaching and activities that Jesus was familiar with urban life. We are in a position to see these indications more clearly because of the excavations that have taken place in Galilee.

While the Gospels say nothing of a visit to Sepphoris, Jesus may have alluded to the prominent, elevated city in a well-known saying, 'A city set on a hill cannot be hid' (Matt. 5.14). The saying that immediately follows, 'Nor do people light a lamp and put it under a bushel, but on a stand' (Matt. 5.15; Mark 4.21; Luke 8.16; 11.33), suggests that the reason a city on a hill cannot be hid is that its light, especially at night, is seen from a distance. A well-lit Sepphoris would have been visible to the people of nearby Nazareth.

Figure 1.5 First-century Capernaum
Excavations of first-century Capernaum have uncovered floors, foundations and lower portions of the walls of various buildings and private homes. The dark stone is volcanic basalt. The limestone synagogue in the background dates to a later time.

Jesus set up his headquarters, as it were, in the large village – or small city? – of Capernaum on the northwest shore of the Sea of Galilee. Excavations at this site have uncovered the volcanic basalt footings of a public building (Figure 1.5), probably the original synagogue (the partly reconstructed limestone synagogue that now rests on the footings dates no earlier than the third century CE).[10] A private home, converted into a public meeting place and still later expanded into an octagonal church, has also been excavated. Although not certain, this may well have been the home of Peter or his mother-in-law in which Jesus taught and in which he was sought out by crowds (Mark 1.21–34).[11] Not too far from the synagogue are ruins that have been tentatively identified as those belonging to a military official and a number of soldiers. Although the Gospels call this man a 'centurion' (Matt. 8.5; Luke 7.2; John 4.46, 49 – where

31

he is a 'royal official'), he probably was not a Roman but an officer under the authority of the tetrarch Antipas, who employed Roman terminology. The Roman bath and remains of other structures that may have been Roman date to the second century.[12]

In relocating to Capernaum, Jesus placed himself in the vicinity of important trade routes and lines of communication, so it isn't surprising that word of what Jesus does in Capernaum becomes known throughout Galilee (Mark 1.28, 32–33, 37, 45; Luke 4.23: 'what we have heard you did at Capernaum'). Before long Jesus is hard-pressed by large crowds (Mark 3.20; 4.1; 6.53–56); he even seeks solitary places where he can be alone (Mark 3.7–10; 6.30–33, 45–46).

Given its location it isn't surprising that there was a customs office in Capernaum. It was here that Jesus called Levi the tax collector (Mark 2.14; Luke 5.27), also known as Matthew (Matt. 9.9; 10.3), who hosted a reception at which a number of other tax collectors and 'sinners' were present (Mark 2.15–17; Luke 5.29–32; Matt. 9.10–13). Jesus becomes known for associating with tax collectors (Luke 7.29; 15.1; 19.2) and he often refers to tax collectors in his teaching (Matt. 11.19; 18.17; 21.31–32; Luke 18.10–14). Associations with and references to tax collectors reflect an urban element.

Jesus warns his disciples to come to terms with those who threaten legal action, lest they be dragged into court and perhaps thrown into prison (Matt. 5.25–26). Courts and prisons are located in cities, not small villages. In this connection one thinks of Jesus' parable of the Indifferent Judge who gives in to the nagging widow (Luke 18.1–8).

Jesus exhorts his disciples to enter the 'narrow gate', not the 'broad gate', which leads to death (Matt. 7.13–14). Although the saying is metaphorical and moral, the image is that of city gates, which in turn implies walled cities, not rural villages. Jesus' lament that his generation is like the children piping and singing in the 'market places' (Matt. 11.16–19; Luke 7.31–35) makes better sense in reference to a city rather than a village setting.[13]

Some of Jesus' parables reflect urban life and the commercial realities that go with it. The parable of the labourers (Matt. 20.1–16) imagines a number of unemployed men loitering in the 'market place'. First-century readers would likely assume that these day labourers have lost their land to wealthy landholders and commercial farmers. Many of these owners of large farms would have lived in nearby cities. The same probably applies in the case of the parable of the Wicked Vineyard Tenants (Mark 12.1–12). The tenant vine-dressers are under contract with an absentee owner and, as the story in the parable shows, they are resentful and desire to acquire the vineyard for themselves. And finally one thinks of the parable of the Dishonest Steward (Luke 16.1–9) whose accounts with his master's debtors reflect a substantial business the transactions and records of which would have been imagined as taking place in an urban rather than a rural setting.[14]

Return to Nazareth

If Sepphoris, the largest city in the vicinity of Nazareth, was thoroughly Jewish in the time of Jesus, as the archaeology of the last 20 years suggests, then what may we conclude with respect to Nazareth itself? It is very probable that a small Jewish village like Nazareth would have been very devout.

As it happens, what little the New Testament Gospels tell us about Nazareth suggests that the villagers were both devout and quite conservative. When Jesus preached in Nazareth, his hometown, his reception was anything but cordial. The Markan evangelist simply says, 'And on the sabbath he began to teach in the synagogue' (Mark 6.2).[15] Nothing is said about what he taught. Luke tells us that Jesus recited part of Isaiah 61 ('The Spirit of the Lord is upon me, because he has anointed me to preach good news') and then declared that 'this scripture is fulfilled' (Luke 4.18–21). Luke's expanded version likely captures the essence of Jesus' teaching, namely the good news of the rule of God (Mark 1.15). Although the reaction is initially and briefly positive, at least as Luke tells the story (Luke 4.22), the mood of the villagers sours quickly.

The villagers apparently had no objection to sabbath sermons devoted to the good news of God's rule, but they evidently didn't think Jesus possessed the credentials to make such an announcement; either that or they didn't like the way Jesus understood and applied this good news. The first option appears to be the understanding of the evangelists Matthew and Mark. According to them the people of Nazareth ask:

> Where did this man get all this? What is the wisdom given to him? What mighty works are wrought by his hands! Is not this the carpenter, the son of Mary and brother of James and Joses and Judas and Simon, and are not his sisters here with us?
>
> (Mark 6.2–3; see also Matt. 13.54–55)

The last question, which refers to Jesus' trade ('carpenter'), his personal identification ('son of Mary') and his brothers and sisters, borders on contempt. In fact it is too offensive for the evangelist Matthew, who revises part of the question to read, 'Is not his mother called Mary?' (Matt. 13.55). Mark's simpler 'son of Mary' (instead of the more conventional 'son of Joseph') could well have alluded to uncertainty about Jesus' conception; that is, who his father was. Matthew will have none of that (and, of course, in his infancy narrative has explained that Jesus was conceived by the Holy Spirit and was raised by Joseph as his son). These rhetorical questions imply that Jesus lacked the qualifications to make weighty pronouncements, such as the arrival of the rule of God and the fulfilment of scriptural prophecies. Because Jesus is one of them, so the villagers reason, there is nothing special about him. In response to this scepticism Jesus declares, 'A prophet is not without honour, except in his own country, and among his own kin, and in his own house' (Mark 6.4).

The version presented in Luke offers a different explanation for the rejection of Jesus. Although happy enough to hear that the prophecy of Isaiah has been fulfilled, even as it was spoken (Luke 4.21, literally: 'Today this scripture is fulfilled in your ears'), the congregation is deeply offended by the suggestion that the good news of the rule of God will benefit Gentiles, even enemies of Israel, as exemplified in the activities of the famous prophets of old, Elijah and Elisha (Luke 4.25–27). Reference to these prophets would have been especially arresting given that they were from the northern kingdom of Israel, what in the time of Jesus is Galilee. Moreover these prophets were famous for their deeds, not their writings. They healed people (2 Kings 5.8–14), raised the dead (1 Kings 17.17–24; 2 Kings 4.29–37; 13.20–21) and even multiplied loaves (2 Kings 4.42–44). Elijah was even associated with the coming day of the Lord (Mal. 4.5: 'Behold, I will send you Elijah the prophet before the great and terrible day of the Lord comes'; see also Sir. 48.10). In many ways these famous prophets, 'local heroes' in the eyes of the Galileans, were models for Jesus himself. As they had done, so Jesus healed people and, like Elijah, proclaimed the eschatological hour.

The conviction that the prophecy of Isaiah 61 was for the righteous of Israel alone is not a guess; it is documented thanks to a fragmentary scroll found near Qumran. According to 11Q13, also called the Melchizedek Scroll, the mysterious figure Melchizedek (see Gen. 14.17–20; Ps. 110.4) will come in fulfilment of Isaiah 61.1–3 ('the Lord has anointed me to bring good tidings to the afflicted; he has sent me to bind up the brokenhearted, to proclaim liberty to the captives'). He will not only liberate Israel and forgive Israel her sins, he will destroy Satan (or Belial) and those allied with him; that is, Israel's enemies. If the interpretation of Isaiah 61 in 11Q13 is anything to go by, we should assume that the people of Nazareth believed that the anointed of the Lord, foretold in the prophecy, would bring blessings to Israel and judgement upon Israel's enemies. If Jesus of Nazareth was the fulfilment of Isaiah 61 (that is, the messenger anointed of God to bring the good news of the day of the Lord's favour), then surely this means blessing for the people of Nazareth and payback for their enemies. But Jesus' interpretation of Isaiah's prophecy, in which he appealed to the examples of the prophets Elijah and Elisha, hinted at something else.

Outraged at Jesus for suggesting that the good news was as much for Israel's enemies as for Israel, the men of the synagogue thrust him out of the village and 'led him to the brow of the hill on which their city was built, that they might throw him down headlong' (Luke 4.29). Although no one knows which 'brow of the hill' the evangelist had in mind (only modern tour guides seem to know!), the description fits the topography of Nazareth and its immediate environs.

Both Gospel versions of the unhappy Nazareth visit are consistent with what we know of this village, from the little archaeology that has been done and from what we can infer from the larger context of Galilee itself. We have in this story a reflection of the mindset of the inhabitants of a small Galilean village, in an environment that takes seriously its Jewish heritage and longs for the fulfilment of the prophecies found in sacred Scripture. To the extent that local prophets of old, such as Elijah and Elisha, forecast things to come and so had any relevance for contemporary Galilean Jews, it was believed that they augured future blessings. But these blessings are for God's people – for Israel, not for outsiders, Gentiles and certainly not Israel's enemies. And no local man – and that includes a carpenter whose family is well known to all in the village – is in any position to say otherwise.

What we have observed in the two accounts of Jesus' visit to his hometown is not the first hint of tension between Jesus and the people of Nazareth. At the very beginning of his ministry we are told that Jesus left Nazareth and 'went and dwelt in Capernaum by the sea' (Matt. 4.13). Why did Jesus relocate to Capernaum? Were the dynamics seen in his visit to the synagogue already in play, even at the outset of his public ministry? There is yet another and more obvious incident in which we see tension between Jesus and his family. It is not clear where precisely this story takes place; perhaps we should assume Capernaum. In any case, we are told that when Jesus learned that his mother and brothers were seeking him, he replied: 'Here are my mother and my brothers! Whoever does the will of God is my brother, and sister, and mother' (Mark 3.34–35; Matt. 12.48–50; Luke 8.21). No matter how this story is nuanced, it clearly testifies to some tension between Jesus and his family.

We cannot be precisely sure of the cause of this tension, but the accounts of the preaching at the synagogue may provide us with an important clue. Jesus' family, along with most of the inhabitants of Nazareth, did not think that he – one of their own – was qualified to announce the good news of the rule of God, and certainly not to challenge their understanding of the implications of the rule of God for themselves and others. After all, one of Jesus' first followers was remembered to have asked, 'Can anything good come out of Nazareth?' (John 1.45). Perhaps it's no surprise that the people of Nazareth had doubts about Jesus and that even his own brothers didn't believe in him, at least initially (John 7.5).

In this chapter we have touched on Jesus in the synagogue. I've suggested that the synagogue is the context in which Jesus' development and religious thought should be understood, not in an imagined urban setting – nearby Sepphoris for example – where Jesus might have come under the influence of Greek philosophy. In the next chapter the synagogue will be explored further. What archaeological evidence is there for synagogues in the time of Jesus? And if they existed, what did they look like and what was their function?

2

Among the devout: religious formation in the synagogue

Readers of the New Testament Gospels are left with the impression that Jesus frequented the synagogue, a place where the Jewish people gathered for prayer and the reading of Scripture; that visiting synagogues was part of his routine. For example, the evangelist Matthew says: 'And he went about all Galilee, teaching in their synagogues and preaching the gospel of the kingdom and healing every disease and every infirmity among the people' (Matt. 4.23). Similarly the evangelist Luke notes, almost in passing, that Jesus 'went to the synagogue, as his custom was, on the sabbath day' (Luke 4.16). In a more apologetic tone, the Johannine Jesus declares: 'I have always taught in synagogues and in the temple, where all Jews come together' (John 18.20). The book of Acts depicts the early Church either existing within or in various ways engaged with the synagogue. Thus even with the founding of the Christian Church in the aftermath of Easter, the Jewish synagogue continues to play an important role.

The word 'synagogue' appears more than 50 times in the Gospels and Acts. Originally, from the Greek meaning 'gathering [of people]' or 'gathering [place]', it referred to groups of people; later also the building in which they gathered. Most of the New Testament occurrences are in reference to buildings where Jewish people gather to pray, worship, read Scripture and socialize. In Israel a small number of buildings that date before 70 CE have been identified as synagogues, as well as a larger number from later times in Israel and elsewhere.

Did synagogue buildings exist in the time of Jesus?

About 15 years ago Howard Clark Kee, a distinguished professor of the New Testament, published a series of studies arguing that all the references to synagogues in the Gospels and Acts were anachronistic, including references to synagogue buildings in the writings of Josephus (*c.*37–100 CE), the Jewish apologist and historian who survived the great Jewish rebellion (66–70 CE). Kee insisted that there were no synagogue buildings prior to 70 CE, the year the temple of Jerusalem was destroyed. Only after this destruction did synagogue buildings begin to appear, to compensate for the loss of the temple. Not only was all first-century literary evidence rejected, Kee also dated the Jerusalem synagogue inscription to a time well after 70 and suggested that pre-70 synagogue buildings identified by archaeologists are not synagogues at all.[1] Almost no one agrees with these negative findings.[2] Nevertheless, it is necessary and helpful to review the evidence.

I begin with the literary evidence outside the New Testament. In at least three places Josephus refers to 'synagogues', which can only be understood as buildings and not simply as gatherings of people:

> The Jews in Caesarea had a synagogue adjoining a plot of ground owned by a Greek of that city; this site they had frequently endeavoured to purchase offering a price far exceeding its true value ... On the following day, which was a sabbath, ... the Jews assembled at the synagogue.　　　　　　　　　　　　　　　　(*J.W.* 2.285–89)

> Although Antiochus surnamed Epiphanes [175–164 BCE] sacked Jerusalem and plundered the temple, his successors on the throne restored to the Jews of Antioch all such votive offerings as were made of brass, to be laid up in their synagogue ...　　　　(*J.W.* 7.44)

> 'Inasmuch as certain of you have had such mad audacity ... not to obey this edict ... in that you have prevented the Jews from having a synagogue by transferring to it an image of Caesar, you have thereby sinned not only against the law of the Jews, but also against the emperor, whose image was better placed in his own shrine than in that of another, especially in the synagogue; for by natural law each must be lord over his own place, in accordance with Caesar's decree.'
> 　　　　　　　　　　　　　　　　　　　　(*Ant.* 19.305)

The event in the first passage, which describes one of the incidents that instigated the first major war with Rome, took place in 66 CE. The second passage describes events from the Hasmonean period (presumably the second century BCE), while the third summarizes the words of Publius Petronius, governor of Syria, who in 41 CE rebuked the people of Dora for placing an image of Caesar in a synagogue. In all three passages it is quite clear that the word 'synagogue' refers to the *building* in which the Jewish people meet and not simply to the *people* who gather.

Kee responds to this evidence by suggesting that Josephus is speaking anachronistically (much as does the Lukan evangelist, he supposes), by retrojecting post-70 CE Jewish realities, which in the aftermath of the destruction of the temple of Jerusalem now included the building of synagogues as places of worship. This objection, however, amounts to little more than special pleading. Would Josephus, to whom synagogue buildings were an innovation during his lifetime (assuming Kee's hypothesis), retroject them into earlier periods in Israel's history? It seems unlikely. After all, Josephus would have lived on into his middle age without synagogue building (again assuming Kee's hypothesis), so why he did find it necessary to read a recent innovation back into the first half of his life?

However we understand the evidence of Josephus, Kee's hypothesis does not account for usage of 'synagogue' in Philo (*c*.20 BCE – 50 CE), who long before the temple was destroyed – and therefore before the changes Kee envisages took place – had this to say about the Essenes:

> In these they are instructed at all other times, but particularly on the seventh days. For that day has been set apart to be kept holy and on it they abstain from all other work and proceed to sacred places [*hierous topous*], which they call 'synagogues' [*synagōgai*]. There, arranged in rows according to their ages, the younger below the older, they sit decorously as befits the occasion with attentive ears. Then one takes the books and reads aloud and another of especial proficiency comes forward and expounds what is not understood.
>
> (*Quod omnis probus liber sit* 81–82)

In this passage 'synagogues' cannot simply mean 'gatherings' of people but must mean actual places or buildings that were regarded by Essenes as 'sacred places'. What is described here is essentially what all religiously observant Jews did, including seating conventions. In fact in broad outline Philo's description of the proceedings of the Essene synagogue matches the description seen in Luke 4.16–30, where Scripture is read and then expounded (v. 16: 'And he came to Nazareth, where he had been brought up; and he went to the synagogue, as his custom was, on the sabbath day. And he stood up to read'; also vv. 20, 28).

Perhaps most devastating of all for Kee's argument is the inscription from the North African city Berenike (in Cyrenaica), which is especially helpful because it is easily dated.[3] It reads:

> In the second year of the emperor Nero Claudius Caesar Drusus Germanicus, on the 16th of Chorach. It was resolved by the congregation [*synagōgē*] of the Jews in Berenike that [the names of] those who donated to the repairs of the synagogue [*synagōgē*] be inscribed on a stele of Parian marble. (*SEG* XVII 823)

In this inscription we see the Greek word *synagōgē* used in both senses of congregation and building. The reference to the 'second year' of Nero (col. 1, line 1) dates the inscription to 55/56 CE. The reference to the '16th of Chorach' (col. 1, line 2) dates the inscription to 3 December 55. In view of this evidence it seems clear that buildings referred to as 'synagogues' existed prior to 70 CE. Moreover the evidence of Jewish connections between Cyrenaica and Judea[4] increases the probability that the pre-70 CE existence of Jewish synagogues in North Africa corroborates the existence of the same in Judea. Even without the North African inscription there appears to be weighty archaeological evidence for synagogue buildings in Israel in the time of Jesus. I begin with an important inscription.

During excavations in and around Mount Ophel, or the 'City of David', in 1913, Raimund Weill discovered a stone slab measuring 75 cm by 41 cm that had probably served as a foundation stone, bearing what is now usually called the Theodotos Inscription[5] (Figure 2.1). The stone is now housed in the Rockefeller Museum in Jerusalem. This Greek inscription seems to provide concrete evidence of the existence of buildings prior to 70 CE specifically designated as 'synagogues'. It reads:

> Theodotos, [son] of Vettenus, priest and synagogue ruler, son of a synagogue ruler, [and] grandson of a synagogue ruler, built the synagogue for the reading of the law and the teaching of the commandments, and the guest room, and the chambers, and the water fixtures, as an inn for those in need from foreign parts, (the synagogue) which his fathers and the elders and Simonides founded. (*CIJ* no. 1404)

Figure 2.1 Theodotos inscription
The Jerusalem synagogue inscription that mentions one 'Theodotos, (son) of Vettenus, priest and synagogue ruler'. The inscription dates to a generation or so before the destruction of Jerusalem in 70 CE. Photograph courtesy of Anders Runesson.

Objections to the pre-70 CE dating of the Theodotos inscription have been set forth in the aforementioned studies by Howard Kee. He has argued that because there is no evidence for synagogue buildings prior to 70 and because references to synagogues as buildings in the New Testament (especially in Luke–Acts) are anachronistic, the Theodotos inscription should be dated to a later time, perhaps as late as the third or fourth century. He claims that the style of engraving in the inscription is from a later time, not from the Herodian period as almost all archaeologists thought.

We have seen that Kee's literary arguments for the non-existence of synagogue buildings prior to 70 CE are weak. After all, Philo, writing some time around 40 CE – 30 years before the destruction of the Jerusalem temple – speaks of synagogue buildings. We have also noted the dated North African inscription, which confirms the existence of synagogue buildings, at least in nearby North Africa, prior to 70.

In any case, Kee's late-dating of the Theodotos inscription on the basis of palaeography is not persuasive. Experienced archaeologists, palaeographers and epigraphers almost unanimously agree that the orthography of the inscription matches the Herodian style (as seen, for example, in comparison with the orthography of the temple warning inscription or the temple donation inscription (*SEG* XXXIII 1277), both of which are pre-70), not the post-70 style.[6]

What I find especially persuasive is the stratigraphy of the find. The inscription was apparently found in a cistern amid rubble possibly from the 70 CE destruction of Jerusalem (though there is some doubt about this). The stones and debris may have been cast away during repairs and reconstruction of Jerusalem in the aftermath of the Bar Kokhba Revolt (132–5 CE). This is what one would expect if the inscription were part of a building damaged or destroyed in 70 and partially cleared away for later building activities. If the inscription had adorned a third- or fourth-century synagogue, one wonders how it could have been disturbed by early second-century construction. Furthermore, there is no evidence that the Ophel area of Jerusalem was inhabited during the second, third and fourth centuries, when Kee imagines the Theodotos synagogue to have existed.[7] The lack of habitation during the second to fourth centuries strongly argues a first-century date for the inscription – as almost all palaeographers have concluded – and the synagogue building of which it was a part.

Are there literary references to the Theodotos synagogue? Possibly. A few scholars identify the synagogue mentioned in Acts 6.9 – 'some of those who belonged to the synagogue of the Freedmen (as it was called), and of the Cyrenians' – with the synagogue mentioned in the Theodotos inscription. Although not impossible, the identification is speculative and is rejected by many.

The importance of the Theodotos inscription, securely dated to the first half of the first century, is in its corroboration of the existence of synagogue buildings in the time of Jesus, just as the Gospels and Acts narrate. Even if we assume that the Theodotos inscription was erected only a few years before the outbreak of the rebellion in 66 CE, the description of Theodotos as the 'grandson of a synagogue ruler' dates at least one synagogue as far back as the time of Jesus, if not further.

The Theodotos inscription also attests the title of 'synagogue ruler' (*archisynagōgos*) in the period before 70 CE. Here again one immediately thinks of the desperate Jairus, one of the 'rulers of the synagogue', who sought from Jesus help for his dying daughter (Mark 5.21–24, 35–43), or the unnamed ruler of the synagogue who criticized him for healing on the sabbath (Luke 13.10–17). The grandfather of Theodotos would have been a contemporary – probably an older contemporary – of the synagogue rulers mentioned in the Gospels.

In Acts, synagogues (6.9; 9.2, 10; 13.5; *passim*) and synagogue rulers (13.15; 18.8, 17) continue to be mentioned (see also Justin Martyr, *Dialogue with Trypho* 137). We also encounter those whom the Lukan evangelist calls 'God-fearers' (*sebesthai ton theon*) or 'devout persons' (*sebomenoi*). For examples, see Acts 16.14 ('a woman named Lydia . . . a worshipper of God') and 17.17 ('he argued in the synagogue with the Jews and the devout persons'). There is mention of God-fearers in connection with synagogues in the Diaspora. We have an example of this in an inscription from the theatre of Miletus (discovered by Theodor Wiegand in 1906), which reads: 'Place of the Jews, who are also called "God-fearers"' (*CIJ* no. 748).

From time to time the author of Acts refers to 'God-fearing' proselytes or Gentiles (13.43, 50; 16.14; 17.4, 17; 18.7, 13). In one passage he refers to one 'Titius Justus, a worshipper of God' (18.7: 'And he left there and went to the house of a man named Titius Justus, a worshipper of God; his house was next door to the synagogue'). One of the cities that Paul visited was Miletus (Acts 20.15, 17).

Taken together, the evidence for the existence of synagogue buildings where Jews, proselytes, God-fearers and synagogue rulers met for prayer, reading of Scripture and social activities is quite substantial. But it also needs to be emphasized that the buildings that have been identified as 'synagogues' served a variety of purposes and were not exclusively religious (as would be the case in later times). Excavations of a number of synagogues in Israel have provided further evidence of their existence prior to 70 CE, as well as some insight into their function, which in turn may help us better understand the activities of Jesus.

Pre-70 synagogues of Israel

The North African inscription and the Theodotos inscription of Jerusalem provide compelling epigraphal evidence of the existence of synagogue buildings prior to the time of the destruction of Jerusalem in 70 CE. Reference in the Theodotos inscription to a grandfather, who was also a ruler of the synagogue, argues strongly for the existence of the synagogue at least as far back as the 20s, or to the time of Jesus himself. The literary evidence is also strong and uniform. Besides the many references to synagogues in the New Testament Gospels and Acts, both Philo and Josephus speak of synagogue buildings in the time of Jesus, if not earlier. And, of course, eight or nine buildings have been identified as synagogues and have been dated to times prior to 70. To these buildings we now turn.

Most archaeologists now speak of eight or nine synagogues that date to the pre-70 era. These include Capernaum, Gamla, the Herodium, Jericho, Magdala, Masada, Modi'in, Qiryat Sefer and Shuafat.[8] Two buildings – Capernaum and Shuafat – are in doubt; the other seven are not. The Jerusalem synagogue attested by the Theodotos inscription is not included in the survey below because the ruins of the synagogue themselves have not been found. A few of these synagogues are also mentioned in our literary sources, chiefly Josephus and the New Testament Gospels.

Capernaum

In Chapter 1 it was noted that Jesus established his base of operations in Capernaum, where we are told there was a synagogue. Within the Gospels we have independent traditions of Jesus' activities in a synagogue in Capernaum. In the Synoptic Gospels Jesus is confronted by a man 'with an unclean spirit' (Mark 1.21–28; Luke 4.31–38). Because of Jesus' remarkable success in casting out the spirit ('With authority he commands even the unclean spirits, and they obey him!'), we are told that 'at once his fame spread everywhere throughout all the surrounding region of Galilee' (Mark 1.28). The exorcism's taking place in a public setting, such as the synagogue, and in a large village like Capernaum, strategically located with respect to trade and travel routes, facilitated the rapid spread of Jesus' reputation.

The Q tradition – the teaching of Jesus shared by Matthew and Luke, not derived from Mark – also references the Capernaum synagogue. A 'centurion' – probably an officer under the authority of tetrarch Antipas rather than Rome – petitions Jesus on behalf of a seriously ill servant (Matt. 8.5–13; Luke 7.1–10). Jewish elders speak to Jesus in support of this man, saying that 'he loves our nation, and he built our synagogue' (Luke 7.5). Matthew's version of the story, as well as the independent version found in John 4.45–54, says nothing about a synagogue. Did Luke add the detail about the synagogue or did Matthew omit it? Matthew may have omitted the Jewish delegation, including reference to the synagogue (Luke 7.3–6a), because of the addition of the saying about those from afar who will sit with the patriarchs (Matt. 8.11–12), which was also drawn from Q elsewhere (Luke 13.28–30). *Jewish* elders supporting the centurion's request would have blunted the force of the contrast between those from afar who sit with the patriarchs and those from Israel itself who are cast out.

There is a third mention of the Capernaum synagogue in John 6. After Jesus feeds the multitude, he crosses the sea and returns to Capernaum. Crowds follow him there and he teaches them about the bread. When the discourse ends the evangelist says, 'This he said in the synagogue, as he taught at Capernaum' (John 6.59).

We may have a fourth reference to the Capernaum synagogue in the story of Jairus and his dying daughter (Mark 5.21–24, 35–43). Capernaum is not named but it is probably the place where Jesus and his disciples make landfall after crossing the Sea of Galilee. The desperate father is Jairus and he is said to be 'one of the rulers of the synagogue' (Mark 5.22, 36, 38). If the synagogue of Capernaum is in view, then we know that there were at least two men of this synagogue who were recognized as synagogue 'rulers'.

The archaeological evidence for a first-century CE (or earlier) synagogue at Capernaum is less than certain. The impressive limestone synagogue through which tourists today wander dates to the third or fourth century (Figures 2.2 and 2.3). But as noted in Chapter 1, excavations have revealed a black basalt foundation beneath the limestone synagogue (Figure 2.4). Is this foundation the remains of an older synagogue? Answers differ. Some think that the basalt foundation was the foundation of a first-century CE or BCE synagogue, others that it was originally part of one or more private residences.[9]

Although far from certain, I think the older basalt foundation is indeed the foundation of the older synagogue, which is probably the

Figure 2.2 Capernaum columns 1
The interior of the fourth-century limestone synagogue at Capernaum.

synagogue mentioned in three, perhaps four stories in the Gospels. I say this because of the shabbiness of the basalt foundation. It is out of square and, far worse, not level. When one faces the side of the synagogue, with the front and entrances to the right, one will notice that the basalt foundation slopes downward from left to right. To compensate for this slope, the builders of the limestone synagogue had to prepare stones in the first tier that increase in depth from left to right, stone by stone. The stonemasons did a remarkable job, making the new foundation level. Why did the builders of the limestone synagogue go to this trouble? Why did they not replace the sloping, out-of-square foundation with a proper foundation?

The answer is found in the Jewish tradition of building upon a sacred foundation – standing on the shoulders of those who went before us, as we might say. The apostle Paul alludes to this idea when he speaks of Christ as the foundation on which he and other leaders

Figure 2.3 Capernaum columns 2
Massive, ornate interior columns in the fourth-century limestone synagogue at Capernaum. Photograph courtesy of Ginny Evans.

in the Church build (1 Cor. 3.10–15). One must build on this foundation – and take care how one does so. Paul – or one of his students – says something similar in the letter to the Ephesians when he describes the Church as 'built upon the foundation of the apostles and prophets, Christ Jesus himself being the cornerstone' (Eph. 2.19–20; CD 7.17).

This explains why the builders of the limestone synagogue chose to build upon the sloping, out-of-square basalt foundation – it was the foundation of the older synagogue. Although from an engineer's point of view this foundation was defective and should have been replaced, from a religious point of view it was sacred and was to be respected. Upon it the new synagogue would be built. (Would the foundation of a non-religious building command this level of respect? It seems unlikely.) Islam, it may be noted, continued the practice of building on holy sites, for a number of mosques are built over churches and synagogues.

Figure 2.4 Capernaum synagogue wall
The fourth-century limestone synagogue at Capernaum rests on an older (perhaps first century BC) black basalt foundation, probably the foundation of the original synagogue, which Jesus would have visited often.

If this interpretation of the older basalt foundation is correct, then we know the location of the first-century synagogue in which Jesus taught and healed while he was in Capernaum. More will be said about the floor plan, furnishings and seating in the descriptions that follow.

Gamla

Perched on a camel-shaped saddle (the Aramaic *gamla* means 'camel') in the Golan Heights, the lights of the city of Gamla (or Gamala) at night were visible to the people living below around the shores of the Sea of Galilee. Like Sepphoris, the saying about the city on a hill that cannot be hid (Matt. 5.14) could also apply to Gamla.

First-century Jewish historian and apologist Josephus – alias Joseph bar Matthias – described Gamla as a rugged, descending spur in the Golan Mountains that rises to a hump ('so that in form the ridge resembles a camel') surrounded on three sides by 'inaccessible ravines' (*J.W.* 4.1–8). After spirited resistance to the Roman assault, the city was captured and largely destroyed (*J.W.* 4.17–83). It lay undisturbed until archaeological excavations in the 1970s. The synagogue is rectangular, measuring 25 metres in length and 17 metres in width (Figure 2.5). The interior walls are lined with stone benches for seating. The interior is also lined with columns in front of and parallel to the benches (six by length, on each side, and four by width, front and rear).[10] This architectural pattern is common to buildings identified as synagogues before and after 70 CE and is a major factor in such identification.[11]

There is no doubt that this synagogue dates before 70 CE for the city was destroyed by the Romans in November 67, and all the artefacts

Figure 2.5 Gamla synagogue (2009)
The synagogue excavated at Gamla. Photograph courtesy of Anders Runesson.

uncovered in the excavation are consistent with a pre-70 date. Moreover the coins that were unearthed range in date from the reign of the Seleucid Syrian king Antiochus I Soter (*c*.280 BCE) to coins minted by the Roman procurator Antonius Felix (*c*.52–60 CE), plus a few overstruck rebel coins bearing the legend 'for the redemption of holy Jerusalem'. Archaeologists date the synagogue to the second half of the first century BCE, though even earlier dates have been suggested. Adjacent to the synagogue is a ritual bath, or *miqveh* (singular of *miqva'ot*). This plastered, stepped pool was supplied with rain water from the synagogue's roof.

The Herodium

The Herodium (or Herodion) is a round fortress on top of a cone-shaped hill, situated about 12 kilometres south of Jerusalem. Herod had fought a desperate but successful battle against his Parthian-backed rival Antigonus in 40 BCE (Josephus, *J.W.* 1.265; *Ant.* 14.359–60). To commemorate this battle and to take advantage of its strategic location, Herod built a luxurious fortress that in time would become known as the Herodium. During the first great revolt (66–70), rebels seized control of the Herodium (*J.W.* 4.518, 555). Eventually the Romans recaptured it (*J.W.* 7.163).

In the nineteenth century the Herodium was explored by British and French travellers and adventurers. In the 1960s Italian archaeologist Virgilio Corbo conducted four seasons of excavations, work continued by Israeli archaeologist Gideon Foerster. From the 1970s to the present, excavations have been carried out by Ehud Netzer, who only a few years ago uncovered what he thinks is the lost tomb of Herod the Great.[12]

Excavations have revealed that the rebels converted a dining room (or *triclinium*) into a synagogue (Figure 2.6). The room measures 15 metres in length and 10 metres in width. Using building materials from the palace, the rebels constructed two tiers of benches along the walls, as well as interior pillars. The pattern is similar to what is seen at Gamla. There is also a *miqveh* near the entrance to the synagogue. The construction of this makeshift synagogue took place in 66 or 67. The conversion of the dining room attests the widespread recognition among Palestinian Jews of what a synagogue should look like. After all, if a synagogue was no more than a room

Figure 2.6 Herodium synagogue
A makeshift synagogue within the Herodium, constructed by rebels during the 66–73 CE Jewish revolt. Originally the room was a dining hall. One should note the stepped bench seating and the interior columns. Photograph courtesy of Anders Runesson.

large enough for a gathering of people, why would physical alterations, such as those seen at the Herodium, be necessary? The same will be seen at Masada.

Jericho

Excavations have been going on in and around the various sites identified as Jericho for most of the twentieth century. Work continues to this day. In 1998 Ehud Netzer excavated part of the Hasmonean palace at Jericho, uncovering the remains of a building he identified as a synagogue.[13] The building complex is dated from 80 to 74 BCE – it was destroyed completely by the earthquake of 31 BCE. Although some have questioned the identification of this building as a synagogue, suggesting instead that it was a Roman villa, there are synagogue characteristics. These include columns and a *miqveh*.

According to the Gospels, Jesus passed through Jericho on his way to Jerusalem. Luke narrates a story about his meeting and dining with a tax collector (Luke 19.1–10). As Jesus departs Jericho he is petitioned by a blind man (Mark 10.46–52; Luke 18.35–43; blind *men* according to Matt. 20.29–34). The evangelists do not mention a synagogue.

Magdala

In the 1970s Virgilio Corbo announced that he had found the remains of an early first-century BCE building that had served as a synagogue and then later was converted into a springhouse – built over a spring to keep milk and perishables cool – in the first century CE. Ehud Netzer and others challenged Corbo's interpretation, arguing that the building served as a springhouse from the beginning. This challenge has been confirmed by the dramatic 2009 discovery by archaeologists Dina Avshalom-Gorni and Arfan Najar of the building that was Magdala's synagogue (Figure 2.7). James Strange, Anders Runesson and others have since visited the site and confirmed that this building was indeed the synagogue of ancient Magdala.[14] The floor plan is rectangular (though barely – it is almost square, comprising some 120 square metres), with bench seating and interior columns. A stone relief exhibiting a menorah has also been found, which makes it the first of its kind found in pre-70 CE Galilee (Figure 2.8).

What link, if any, Jesus may have had with Magdala and its small synagogue would probably have been through a prominent female follower, Mary Magdalene. This woman is mentioned some dozen times in the Gospels, mostly in reference to Jesus' death, burial and resurrection. Luke tells us that 'Mary, called Magdalene' was among certain women whom Jesus had healed (Luke 8.2). The name 'Magdalene' means one from Magdala (just as 'Nazarene' means one from Nazareth). Given Magdala's proximity to the centre of Jesus' activities in Galilee and around the Sea of Galilee, I should think it is probable that on at least one occasion Jesus visited this village and its synagogue.

Figure 2.7 Migdal site (2010)
A first-century synagogue was recently discovered at Magdala (Hebrew: Migdal), near the Sea of Galilee, the hometown of Mary Magdalene. Excavation and study continue. Photograph courtesy of Anders Runesson.

Masada

Masada (perhaps from Aramaic *metsad*, meaning 'fortress') is the name of a prominent, flat-topped rock cliff overlooking the southern western shore of the Dead Sea. On it Herod built a palace, fortress and series of buildings. Cisterns and an aqueduct from the nearby cliffs to the west supplied this complex with water. It is accessed by a steep, narrow, winding path on the east side, appropriately dubbed the 'Snake Path'. One of the most impressive features is the northern palace, descending in three levels from the northern tip of the rock cliff. Most of Herod's expansion and improvement of Masada took place between 37 and 31 BCE (Josephus, *J.W.* 7.300).

Figure 2.8 Magdala Stone
A stone relief recovered from the first-century Magdala synagogue
depicting the seven-branch menorah with columns on the left and right,
probably representing the Jerusalem temple. Photograph courtesy of
Anders Runesson.

Through cunning and skill the rebels, under the leadership of
Menahem, captured Masada in 66 CE. After Menahem's assassination
in Jerusalem, his nephew Eleazar ben Yair fled to Masada and became
the leader of the rebels and their families who assembled there. While
living at Masada the rebels built a synagogue. In 74 CE Masada was
retaken by the Romans under the command of the general Flavius
Silva.

Masada was excavated by Yigael Yadin between 1963 and 1965.[15]
The synagogue built by the rebels some time between 66 and 74 CE
is located at the northwest end of the rock cliff, not far from the
northern palace (Figure 2.9). It faces northwest; that is, towards
Jerusalem. The structure is rectangular, measuring 12.5 metres in
length and 10.5 metres in width. Four tiers of mud-plastered benches
line the walls, along with two rows of columns – three on the south

Figure 2.9 Masada synagogue
A makeshift synagogue at Masada constructed by rebels during the
66–73 CE Jewish revolt. Again, one should note the stepped bench
seating and the interior columns.

side and two on the north side. A number of Herodian lamps were
found in one corner of the room, along with an ostracon inscribed
'priest's tithe' and fragments of two scrolls (parts of Deuteronomy
and Ezekiel). Elsewhere other fragments of scrolls were found, including biblical, apocryphal and sectarian works.[16]

Modiʻin

During the 2000–1 season at Modiʻin (Khirbet Umm el-ʻUmdan),
about 25 kilometres northwest of Jerusalem, archaeologist Alexander
Onn discovered a synagogue that has been dated to the late Hasmonean
period. It was later modified in the Herodian period. A cistern filled
with broken and unbroken pottery, all of Hasmonean style, assisted
in dating the structure. The synagogue's main room is rectangular,

measuring 12 metres in length and 10 metres in width, with bench seating and columns. A few metres from the synagogue a *miqveh* was also found.[17]

If Khirbet Umm el-'Umdan is indeed the site of Modi'in (or Modein), then the ancestral home of the Hasmonean dynasty may well have been found (1 Macc. 2.1: 'In those days Mattathias the son of John, son of Simeon, a priest of the sons of Joarib, moved from Jerusalem and settled in Modein'; 1 Macc. 2.70: 'He died . . . and was buried in the tomb of his fathers at Modein'; 1 Macc. 9.19; 13.25, 30). Mattathias launched the revolt against Antiochus IV Epiphanes and Seleucid rule in 167 BCE and was succeeded by his sons Judas Maccabeus, Jonathan and Simon. Although in time the Hasmonean dynasty fell out of favour with much of the Jewish public, the valour and deeds of Mattathias and his sons became the stuff of legend.

Excavated synagogues from the time of Jesus	
Locations	*Characteristics (typology)*
Gamla	rectangular floor plan
The Herodium	stepped bench seating along the
Jericho	walls
Magdala	interior columns
Masada	(sometimes) a *miqveh*
Modi'in	(sometimes) portrait of a menorah
Qiryat Sefer	

Qiryat Sefer

Qiryat Sefer (Khirbet Badd 'Isa) is about 25 kilometres north-by-northwest of Jerusalem (and just a few kilometres northeast of Modi'in). The main hall is square, measuring 9.6 metres by 9.6 metres. The stonemasonry is consistent with the Herodian period. There are two rows of stone benches along the eastern and western walls. Stone benches probably lined the southern wall but were looted in antiquity. There are also two rows of plastered, painted columns. The synagogue is dated to the beginning of the first century CE. It was abandoned during the Bar Kokhba Revolt (132–5 CE).[18]

Shuafat

Alexander Onn announced in 1991 that he had found the ruins of a building he identified as a synagogue on Shuafat Ridge, east Jerusalem, that dates to the second century BCE. Onn believes the building was abandoned after the 31 BCE earthquake. Apart from a news report and a few allusions and discrepant descriptions in scholarly literature, nothing major has been published.[19] Anders Runesson has recommended that unless a proper report and documentation are published soon, the claim should be withdrawn.

Jesus and the synagogues

First-century synagogues were probably multi-purpose and were not limited to religious meetings and services only.[20] Most of them in all likelihood served as community centres (to use modern language), as well as places of worship and study. According to rabbinic tradition, most synagogues doubled as schools where Jewish youth were educated. The late Samuel Safrai declares: 'The school was connected with the synagogue according to most Second Temple and later sources. The instruction took place in the prayer hall or in a room adjoining the synagogue.'[21] In support of this claim Safrai can do no better than cite a number of rabbinic texts, most of them dating to the fifth and later centuries CE. His earliest citations are two from the Mishnah (*c.*220 CE), but neither one says anything about schools or synagogues. Safrai in fact does not cite any 'Second Temple' sources (by definition the Second Temple period ends with the destruction of the Herodian temple in 70 CE). Safrai makes a reasonable case for education and literacy in Israel in late antiquity, but none whatever for the presence of schools as such, whether located in synagogues or elsewhere in the first century.

One Second Temple reference that might have been cited is the decree of Caesar Augustus in respect of the rights of the Jewish people outside of the land of Israel. Here is part of the decree, as presented by Josephus:

the Jews may follow their own customs in accordance with the law of their fathers . . . their sacred monies shall be inviolable and may be sent up to Jerusalem and delivered to the treasurers in Jerusalem . . . And if anyone is caught stealing their sacred books [*hieras biblous*] or their sacred monies from a synagogue [*sabbateion*] or a school [*andrōn*], he shall be regarded as sacrilegious, and his property shall be con-fiscated to the public treasury of the Romans.   (*Ant.* 16.163–64)

The text and translation of this interesting passage are uncertain right at the most important place. The word *sabbateion* literally means 'sabbath (building)' in the Greek and Latin manner of speaking (as in the Herodium, or in Greek, the *Herodeion*, the 'Herod [building]'). Josephus and other Jewish authors, so far as I have been able to determine, do not use the word *sabbateion* in reference to a synagogue building, but a Roman or Greek writer might, as we see in Caesar's decree. That *sabbateion* is in reference to a synagogue seems certain in view of the context. The tricky part is the word *andrōn*, which has been translated 'school'. In the standard lexica the word means 'room for men' or 'refectory' (where men eat). In the present context, in which it is paired with *sabbateion*, a 'sabbath (building)', and warning against the theft of 'sacred books', the word *andrōn* prob-ably does refer to a room in which men study Scripture; that is, the 'sacred books' of the Jewish people. Various proposed emendations of the Greek text, including the transliteration *aarōn* (from the Hebrew word meaning 'ark' or closet, in which sacred books are kept), are unnecessary – the text makes sense as it stands. As such it offers a modicum of evidence for schools within synagogues, at least outside the land of Israel.

Whether or not 'schools' functioned within the synagogues of Israel in the time of Jesus, we should assume that the men who attended services and heard Scripture read and interpreted were to some degree being educated. How extensive this education was and how widespread literacy was in Israel in the time of Jesus are questions that will be addressed in Chapter 3. For now it should be acknowledged, first, that there were public buildings – even in villages – that functioned as synagogues in which religious services took place on the sabbath and other days, and second, that these served other public functions, perhaps including education.

Did Jesus attend synagogue services? The Gospels certainly leave us with that impression. The literary as well as circumstantial evidence, including archaeological discoveries, suggest that he attended synagogue services before and during his public ministry. One indication of Jesus' piety from the point of view of his contemporaries is the references to the fringe, or tassels, of his coat. I refer to the story of the woman suffering from a haemorrhage. As Jesus passes by in a throng of people, the woman 'came up behind him, and touched the fringe of his garment' (Matt. 9.20; Luke 8.44). Later in his narrative the evangelist Matthew states that the sick sought Jesus out, 'that they might only touch the fringe of his garment' (Matt. 14.36). The word translated 'fringe' is *kraspedon*, which can also be translated 'tassel'; in Hebrew the tassel is usually in the plural (*zizioth*). The law of Moses commands Torah-observant Jewish males to wear tassels on the borders or corners of their clothing (Num. 15.38–39; Deut. 22.12). Although Jesus himself wears tassels, he is critical of those who 'make . . . their tassels long' because they love to be seen as pious (Matt. 23.5–6). He is not against wearing the sign of fidelity to God's law but opposes sanctimonious ostentation.[22] Archaeology attests the practice of wearing tassels in late antiquity.[23] It is hard to think that whereas Jesus' clothing conformed to pious observation of the Jewish faith, he himself did not attend the synagogue.[24]

There are two more indications that Jesus was familiar with the synagogue of his day. First, he refers to the scribes and Pharisees who 'sit on the seat of Moses' (Matt. 23.2). To what 'Moses' seat' (or chair; the Greek is *kathedra*) refers is much debated. It could be figurative – that is, in the synagogues the scribes and Pharisees *read* the law of Moses; therefore obey what you hear.[25] But the 'seat of Moses' may also refer to an actual chair or seat on which the scribes and rabbis sit when they teach in the schools and synagogues. Special ornate stone seats, complete with Hebrew inscriptions – usually phrases from the Bible – have been found in the ruins of old synagogues at Chorazin (Figure 2.10), Delos, Dura Europos and Hammath-Tiberias, and may be examples of what Jesus mentioned in his criticism of the scribes and Pharisees. In rabbinic literature there are several references to the Seat of Moses.[26] It may be viewed in the narrative of Jesus preaching in the synagogue of Nazareth,

Figure 2.10 Moses' seat, Chorazin
An ornate 'Seat of Moses' from the fourth-century synagogue at Chorazin.

where we are told that he 'stood up to read' from Scripture and then 'sat down' to begin his teaching (Luke 4.16, 20). In all probability the seat on which Jesus sat was called the 'Seat of Moses', even if in his day it was much plainer than the more ornate thrones of later times.

A second indication that Jesus was active in the synagogue, before and during his public ministry, is seen in his paraphrases and interpretations of Scripture, especially the book of Isaiah. What we find is a marked degree of coherence between Jesus' use of Isaiah and the way this book came to be translated, often with much interpretive paraphrasing, in the Aramaic version that came to be called the Targum (see below). For example, in alluding to Isaiah 6.9–10, Jesus concludes with the words, 'and it be forgiven them' (Mark 4.12), as it reads in the Aramaic, instead of 'and I heal them', which is how it reads in the Hebrew. Jesus' saying about perishing by the sword (Matt. 26.52) alludes to the Aramaic paraphrase of Isaiah 50.11. His paraphrase of Isaiah 66.24, in which he adds reference to Gehenna (Mark 9.47–48), again reflects the Aramaic. His understanding of Isaiah 5.1–7, alluded to in some of the details in the parable of the Vineyard (Mark 12.1–9), reflects the Aramaic paraphrase. Jesus' assurance to his disciples that 'after three days' or 'on the third day' he will be raised up (Mark 8.31 for example) probably reflects the interpretive Aramaic paraphrase of Hosea 6.2. His command, 'Be merciful, even as your Father [in heaven] is merciful' (Luke 6.36 = Matt. 5.48), coheres with the interpretive Aramaic expansion of Leviticus 22.28: 'My people, children of Israel, as our Father is merciful in heaven, so shall you be merciful on earth' (*Tg. Ps.-J.*).

The point of all of this is that the Aramaic paraphrase of Scripture developed in the synagogue, orally at first; eventually it was committed to writing and became known as the Targum. Thanks to the discoveries at Qumran and elsewhere near the Dead Sea, we now know that Targums – the plural form can also be 'Targumim' – were written as early as the first century BCE. It is hard to see how Jesus could have absorbed so much material that is consistent with the emerging targumic tradition if he did not frequent the synagogue.

We may ask how well known the Scriptures were in the time of Jesus. How many people could read them? How were books made, circulated and studied? We shall turn to these and related questions in the next chapter.

3

In the books: reading, writing and literacy

In recent years a number of scholars have suggested that Jesus could not read, that in all likelihood none of his disciples could read either. They say this because of studies that have concluded that rates of literacy in the Roman Empire were quite low and that Jesus and his earliest followers were probably not exceptions.[1] There are some problems with this position, not least making judgements about the literacy of Jesus on the basis of what we imagine was the education and literacy of an 'average' Galilean Jew in the first century. The question of the literacy of Jesus will be addressed later in this chapter. We begin with a review of the archaeological evidence for general literacy in late antiquity.

Archaeological evidence for literacy in late antiquity

Evidence for literacy is found, as we would expect, in literature; either in direct claims about who can or cannot read or in what seems to be implied. Writing in the early third century CE, a Roman official orders a number of mayors in the Hermopolite district in Egypt to post copies of his letter 'in the metropolis and in the well-known places . . . so that no one may be unaware of my pronouncements' (P. Oxy. 2705). One is left with the impression that it is expected that most adults will be able to read the official's letter. First-century Jewish historian and apologist Josephus claims that Jewish children were educated and that this education included being taught to read (*Ag. Ap.* 1.60; 2.204). Another Jewish text, written a bit earlier than the time of Josephus, speaks of a man who read Bible stories to his children (4 Macc. 18.11). Other texts, especially from the later literature of the Rabbis, could be cited in which the same claims are made. If these claims were taken at face value, one would conclude that most Jewish males in the time of

Jesus could read. But scholars usually take such assertive generalizations with a grain of salt. Pride, nationalism, hyperbole, apologetics and the like, rather than reality, are suspected to lie behind these statements. If the claims of literature are misleading, what does archaeology tell us?

At first blush archaeological finds seem to tell us the same as the glowing claims in literature – that everybody in the Roman Empire could read. In every city from late antiquity we find dozens, if not hundreds of public inscriptions (see Figure 3.1). These inscriptions are dedications, lists of names, imperial decrees, statements or reminders of law, quotations of famous men and even rather pedestrian things, such as directions. Many gravestones and tombs are inscribed with more than the name of the deceased; some have lengthy, even poetic obituaries; others have threats and curses against grave robbers

Figure 3.1 Milestone, Capernaum
A Roman milestone, inscribed in Latin, found during excavations at Capernaum.

(literate ones, evidently!). The impression one gains is that everybody was expected to be able to read; otherwise, what was the point of all of these expensive inscriptions, incised on stone?

To the inscriptions we must add the enormous numbers of documents from late antiquity that have been found. One thinks especially of the finds at Oxyrhynchus ranging from 300 BCE to 500 CE. Close to half a million documents, mostly made of papyrus, were recovered from the dry sands just outside the city limits. Less than 10 per cent of this discarded 'library' has been published to date. In places the heaps of papyri in the landfills ran as much as 9 metres deep. Most of the papyri recovered were found in the first 3 metres or so, below which the sand was damp from seepage from the nearby canal fed by the River Nile, so that most of the papyri had rotted and could not be recovered (and much of this decomposed papyrus and garbage was scooped up by local farmers and used as fertilizer). In rough terms this could mean that the half-million documents recovered represents only about one-third of those thrown into the dump. One wonders how many millions of other documents circulated in Oxyrhynchus that were never thrown into this dump – and Oxyrhynchus was but one city.

Presumably other cities in the Mediterranean world were every bit as literate as Oxyrhynchus. One thinks of Alexandria (Egypt) and Ephesus (Asia Minor) with their impressive libraries. The former, in its heyday (it was destroyed in the seventh-century Arab conquest), boasted almost half a million volumes (Josephus, *Ant.* 1.10). A nearby temple held another 36,000 books. The Celsus Library at Ephesus had some 12,000. These were larger and more influential cities. If we had access to a large chunk of the documents that their residents pitched into the trash, would the amount be any less than what we have recovered from Oxyrhynchus? What about Corinth, Athens, Rhodes and – by the first century CE – Rome? Recall, too, that Marcus Antonius apparently gave Cleopatra, with whom he was completely besotted, some 200,000 books. Pliny the Elder claims that in preparing to write his *Natural History* he read 2,000 books (*Nat.* Preface §17). There must have been tens of millions, probably hundreds of millions of documents written and read in the Mediterranean world from the time of Alexander until the fall of the Roman Empire.[2]

Surely such great quantities of written material argue for wide-spread not limited literacy? You might think so, but that is not the conclusion historians have reached. Most agree that literacy rates were somewhere between 5 and 10 per cent (and that most of the literate were male), with perhaps somewhat higher rates among the Jewish people. I do not dispute this conclusion.[3] However, if most of the literate were males, then among men literacy rates would be somewhere between 10 and 20 per cent.

Archaeology has provided us with a great number of relevant artefacts, such as examples of quill (whether feather or reed), stylus, inkwell, statues or paintings of scribes (usually seated), abecedaries (that is, practice sheets for beginning scribes), as well as thousands of manuscripts. In late antiquity, writing surfaces included various metals (such as bronze, copper, lead, tin, silver and gold), stone, pottery (ostraca), papyrus (made from the papyrus plant, native to the marshes and banks of the River Nile), parchment and vellum (stretched, treated and rubbed animal skin). Jewish books, especially religious books, tended to be made of parchment and vellum (not conventional tanned leather, which was used for sandals and other tools and implements) rather than papyrus. This was probably because papyrus was imported from Egypt, which may have made it expensive (this point is debated) and certainly would have made it ritually suspect in that it was produced by non-Jews. Home-grown animal hides, which were not ritually suspect and may have been somewhat cheaper, were preferred, as the evidence of the Dead Sea Scrolls makes clear. Of the 900 or so documents recovered from the caves in the vicinity of Qumran, only 100 are made of papyrus; the other 800 or so are made of parchment/vellum (and one of copper).[4]

Funerary statues and portraits depict Egyptian scribes seated, cross-legged, with writing-board in the lap. Jewish scribes may have done the same but there is some evidence that small tables were used for writing and short stools or low benches for sitting. This is seen primarily at the Qumran ruins, where in one room (locus 30), dubbed the 'scriptorium' by excavator Roland de Vaux, were found three inkwells (two made of bronze, one of ceramic; a fourth, also ceramic, was found in the adjacent locus 31), a low table, some five metres in length and half a metre in width, low benches that lined the wall, and the remains of what appear to be two more tables. Although the function of the tables is disputed (whether scribes used them for writing, stacking scrolls or laying out, measuring, cutting and sewing new ones), most agree that the room was used for the production of books.[5]

We have some interesting artefactual evidence of literacy in Italy itself thanks to the eruption of Mount Vesuvius in 79 CE, which buried in hot volcanic ash Pompeii, Herculaneum and a few other nearby villages. One thinks of the well-known painting of the Pompeii couple, bakery owner Terentius Neo and his wife (Figure 3.2).

Figure 3.2 Baker and wife, Pompeii
This remarkable portrait on the wall of a bakery in first-century Pompeii depicts the proprietor holding a bookroll and his wife holding a stylus and a diptych made of two waxed wooden tablets. The stylus tablets are for taking notes; the bookroll represents the finished, polished text. The portrait proclaims the literacy of this otherwise modest couple. Photograph courtesy of www.HolyLandPhotographs.org.

The painting is dated to 15 years or so before the eruption of Vesuvius. Terentius is depicted holding a bookroll and his wife is depicted holding a stylus in her right hand and a diptych of *tabulae ceratae* ('waxed tablets') – that is, a notebook with wax-coated wooden leaves – in her left.[6] The couple, holding their writing implements in a conspicuous manner, evidently wanted to emphasize their literacy – a literacy that included writing as well as reading. Indeed, the wife rests the tip of her stylus against her lower lip and looks thoughtfully into the distance. Her pose is similar to that of a fresco found at Murecine near Pompeii that depicts Calliope, muse of epic poetry. Calliope presses the stylus against her lower lip with her right hand, holds a diptych notebook in her left hand and looks thoughtfully into the distance.[7] The wife of Terentius appears to be mimicking this pose (what might be called the 'Calliope look'), which was fashionable in late antiquity.[8] What is interesting is that this literary couple were not of exalted station, nor were they 'academic' people (philosophers, scribes, authors); they were a bakery-shop owner and his wife! As it so happens, 125 wooden tablets, preserving some 200 pages of text, were discovered in a complex of buildings at Murecine. Most of the tablets are concerned with finance and maritime trade.[9]

The same thing is observed at Vindolanda, the site of a Roman fort and settlement just south of Hadrian's Wall in Northumberland in northern England, where writing tablets were found in 1973 during an excavation conducted by Robin Birley.[10] Some 500 tablets, many in fragments, have been recovered. The tablets are made from local British wood such as alder, birch and oak. There are also examples of tablets made from non-native species of wood, which indicates that some of the tablets were produced elsewhere and imported. Most are diptychs, typically 20 cm by 8 cm, produced by scored and folded wood sheets 0.25–0.30 mm thick, with carbon-based ink writing on the inside. Most of the tablets are letters and reports related to the fortress and military personnel. Several letters are of a private and personal nature. The tablets date from 92 CE to 130 CE, the majority dating before 102 CE. A prominent correspondent was one Flavius Cerialis, prefect of the ninth cohort of Batavians, along with his wife, Sulpicia Lepidina. Tablet 291 is a letter of invitation addressed to Sulpicia by one Claudia Severa, wife of Aelius Brocchus.

Claudia has invited her dear friend to her birthday party: 'Oh how much I want you at my birthday party. You will make the day so much more fun. I do hope you can make it. Goodbye, sister, my dearest soul.'[11] Most of the letter is written in a professional hand, but the closing greetings and signature are in the hand of Claudia herself, making the letter one of the oldest extant Latin writings by a woman. Claudia Severa seems to have been a woman worthy of the Calliope model.

Claudia's hand is in itself of interest. It has been described by a modern epigrapher and Latinist as 'a hesitant, ugly and unpractised hand'. Yet her Latin is 'very elegant'.[12] Claudia was an educated, literate woman. She could read and she could write an elegant Latin, but her penmanship was poor. Her abilities and limitations, however, were not atypical. We see the same in other tablets and in many personal letters among the thousands of papyri documents that have been discovered in Egypt. There are many other examples of professionally written letters, closed with a different, usually clumsy hand and signature. Many Greeks and Romans could read and so should be classified as 'literate', but their writing skills were limited. One's literacy should not be judged on the basis of one's penmanship.

The biggest surprise of the Vindolanda tablets relates to the point just made with regard to Claudia. The tablets provide dramatic evidence of widespread literacy in the Roman army, from equestrian officers whose literacy is not surprising, to low-ranking soldiers, wives, friends, servants and others whose high level of literacy is. The tablets attest to professional, well-practised hands as well as non-professional hands whose penmanship ranges from decent workman-like to barely legible scrawl, marred by misspellings, corrections and strikeouts (indeed, among the tablets are several first and second drafts). If many of the common soldiers could read and write, what does this say about the general literacy of the Roman Empire?[13]

Let us return to Italy and what has been preserved for us thanks to a volcano. For our concerns the biggest find was the excavation of the so-called 'Villa of the Papyri' (*Villa dei Papiri*) in Herculaneum. The villa is halfway up the slope of Mount Vesuvius and was discovered in 1750 by Karl Weber, whose men dug a tunnel, following a mosaic-paved walkway that led them to the villa. From October

1752 to August 1754 Weber and his workers recovered some 1,100 scrolls, a few tablets and broken pieces of both.[14] The scrolls survived because they had been reduced to black carbon by the intense heat of the volcanic eruption. Initial efforts to unroll, disassemble or dissect these scrolls resulted in the destruction of dozens of them. Only small portions of a very few scrolls could be read. The bulk of the discovery has been stored away unread. In recent years scholars have been now in a position to begin reading these scrolls, thanks to multi-spectral imaging and CAT scans (the former technology has been used to good effect in reading what had been unreadable or invisible in some of the Dead Sea Scrolls). For now, we must appreciate the discovery of a private home that contained a library of over 1,000 books.

Before leaving Pompeii we should inquire into the large number of graffiti and what it may imply about literacy. Usually etched into the plaster or paint on walls, in both public and private locations, the graffiti are sometimes humorous, often vulgar and on occasion threatening. Here are a few examples:[15]

In the vestibule of the House of Cuspius Pansa:
'The finances officer of the emperor Nero says this food is poison.'
(*CIL* IV.8075)

On the exterior of the House of Menander:
'Satura was here on September 3rd.' (*CIL* IV.8304)

On the wall of the Bar of Astylus and Pardalus:
'Lovers are like bees in that they live a honeyed life.' (*CIL* IV.8408)

On the wall of the gladiator barracks:
'Floronius, privileged soldier of the 7th legion, was here. The women did not know of his presence. Only six women came to know; too few for such a stallion.' (*CIL* IV.8767)

On the wall of the barracks of the Julian-Claudian gladiators; column in the peristyle:
'Celadus the Thracian gladiator is the delight of all the girls.'
(*CIL* IV.4289)

On the wall of the 'House of the Moralist':
'Remove lustful expressions and flirtatious tender eyes from another man's wife. May there be modesty in your expression.' (*CIL* IV.7698b)

'Postpone your tiresome quarrels if you can, or leave and take them home with you.' (*CIL* IV.7698c)

On the wall of the House of Pascius Hermes; left of the front door: 'To the one defecating here: Beware of the curse. If you look down on this curse, may you have an angry Jupiter for an enemy.' (*CIL* IV.7716)

Perhaps as many as one-third of the graffiti are scatological. A number are curses and more vehement than the one above, evidently inscribed to scare off the person who was using the front porch as a latrine. Two immediately come to mind: 'May you be nailed to the cross!' (*CIL* IV.2082: *in cruce figarus*). Another reads: 'Samius (says) to Cornelius, "Get hung!"' (*CIL* IV.1864: *Samius Cornelio suspendre*). If Pompeii is anything to go by, there must have been hundreds of thousands, perhaps millions of graffiti etched into walls, floors and tombstones in the Mediterranean world. There are many examples in Israel too, though not nearly as 'colourful' as those preserved on the scorched walls of Pompeii and Herculaneum.[16] At the very least these graffiti and inscriptions attest to a crude literacy that reached all levels of society.

One graffito deserves special attention. Although found in Rome, it has a bearing on the fate of Jesus in Jerusalem. The well-known Palatine Graffito was found etched on a plastered wall in what is believed to have been slaves' quarters, perhaps in the *domus Gelotiana*, on the Palatine Hill in Rome.[17] Found in 1857, the graffito has been dated to the first half of the third century.[18] Initially taken to the Kircherian Museum at the Collegio Romano, it is now housed in the Palatine Museum.

The graffito depicts a crucified figure with the head of a donkey (Figures 3.3 and 3.4). The figure's hands and arms are outstretched, evidently nailed to the cross beam[19] or *patibulum*. The figure is wearing a short-sleeved *colobium* or undershirt – the typical dress of slaves – that extends from the shoulders to the waist. The feet rest on a short, horizontal plank. To the left – that is, to the crucified figure's right – is another figure standing, with one arm upraised. The crucified figure is looking at this man. The upraised hand and arm are either a salute or, as one scholar has suggested, the act of throwing a kiss.[20] Between and beneath the two figures, written in

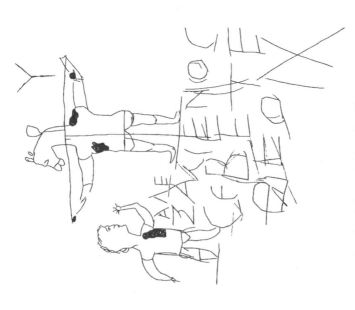

Figure 3.3 Palatine Graffito
The Palatine Graffito (or *Graffito Blasphemo*) depicts a slave worshipping the crucified donkey-headed Jesus. Photograph from Rodolfo Lanciani, *Ancient Rome in the Light of Recent Discoveries* (1898); public domain.

Figure 3.4 Sketch of the Palatine Graffito
This sketch of the Palatine Graffito indicates clearly the figures and the letters. Photograph from Rodolfo Lanciani, *Ancient Rome in the Light of Recent Discoveries* (1898); public domain.

four lines, are the words '*Alexamenos sebete Theon*'. Taken at face value this means, 'Alexamenos, worship God!', but the imperative is unlikely. Most interpreters think that *sebete* is probably a misspelling of the indicative form *sebetai*. Accordingly the words are descriptive: 'Alexamenos worships (his) God'.

However we should interpret the donkey imagery in the graffito, it is interesting that a slave is able to insult a fellow slave by inscribing a written slur on a wall in their quarters. The inscriber's spelling is not perfect and his inscribing work is sloppy (to say nothing of the artwork), but it is clear that he can read and write. In this crude and insulting graffito we have one more indication that literacy was fairly widespread and included persons from all walks of life.

There is also some important archaeological evidence relating to literacy in Israel in late antiquity. In Chapters 1 and 2, Jesus' reading from the prophet Isaiah in the Nazareth synagogue was mentioned. Besides the story in Luke 4.16–30, we may now ask what other evidence is there that books of Scripture were present in the synagogues of Israel? Several times Josephus refers to books kept in the Jerusalem temple (*Ant.* 3.38; 4.303; 5.61), something that Josephus, being of aristocratic priestly heritage, ought to know given his access to the temple complex. After the destruction of the temple, Titus permitted Josephus to take possession of the holy books (*Life* 418). It was noted in Chapter 2 that according to Josephus, Caesar Augustus issued a decree to protect Jewish sacred monies and sacred books stored in their synagogues (*Ant.* 16.163–64).

Elsewhere Josephus refers to Moses' command to the Jewish people to hear the law read to them every sabbath and 'to learn it thoroughly and in detail' (*Ag. Ap.* 2.175). It is implied here that the law of Moses would have been available to the overseer, or 'ruler', of the synagogue. Josephus' older contemporary, Philo, is explicit when he asks his own people rhetorically: 'And would you still sit down in your synagogues, collecting your ordinary assemblies, and reading your sacred volumes in security, and explaining whatever is not quite clear?' (*Dreams* 2.127; see also *Moses* 2.216; *Spec. Laws* 2.62–63). Acts speaks of Scripture being read in the synagogues weekly (13.15, 27; 15.21: 'For from early generations Moses has had in every city those who preach him, for he is read every Sabbath in the synagogues'; 17.2; 18.4). The Rabbis speak of books of Scripture in synagogues of their time (*m. Meg.* 3.6; 4.1). Writing in the middle of the second century, Justin Martyr, an Aramaic-speaking Palestinian Christian, refers to copies of Jeremiah in the synagogues (*Dial.* 72). The existence of numbers of Scripture scrolls is presupposed by the story of Antiochus IV's attempts to confiscate and destroy such scrolls during his pogroms against the Jewish faith (1 Macc. 1.56–57).

There is archaeological evidence that supports if not confirms these literary traditions. Scripture scrolls and related religious and liturgical works were found in or near the makeshift synagogue built by the rebels at Masada. Dozens of Scripture scrolls were uncovered in Qumran's Cave 4, adjacent the buildings in which members of the community worked, studied and, we presume, worshipped. There is evidence that scrolls in Cave 4 were vandalized, perhaps by the Romans who destroyed the compound. By the way: analysis of the scribal hands has shown that most of the scrolls were composed elsewhere in Israel and then brought to Qumran. They attest to a widespread network of scribes and not a small group located in a remote region of Israel.

Another important archaeological find connected to Qumran was the discovery of the earthenware jars, which were fired by the kiln at the Qumran compound and apparently designed to contain and protect the scrolls. This custom did not originate with the men of Qumran; it was an ancient one. It is mentioned in Jeremiah: 'Take these deeds, both this sealed deed of purchase and this open deed, and put them in an earthenware vessel, that they may last for a long time' (Jer. 32.14). There is no better description of the function of the Qumran jars than what we have here. At the beginning of the first century we read in a pseudepigraphal text ascribed to Moses: 'You shall arrange (the scrolls), anoint them with cedar, and deposit them in earthenware jars' (*T. Mos.* 1.16–17). I might also mention the curious story related by the fourth-century church historian and theologian Eusebius. According to him the great Christian biblical scholar Origen of Alexandria (*c.*210 CE) obtained a Scripture scroll 'found at Jericho in a jar' (*Hist. eccl.* 6.16.3). It is possible that this jar had been taken from a cave near Qumran, which is not too far from Jericho. If not, then it demonstrates that the practice of storing biblical scrolls in earthenware jars continued after 70 CE.

Before turning to the specific question of Jesus' literacy, it will be useful to say a few things about what we have learned from the old books that we have found. By this, I mean what we can learn from old books as *artefacts*.

Old books as artefacts

When the discovery of the Great Isaiah Scroll (or 1QIsaiah[a]) was announced in 1948, some wondered if this could have been the very scroll Jesus held and read from in the Nazareth synagogue (Luke 4.16–20). After all, the scroll dates to about 150 BCE and so was an old, well-used scroll even in the time of Jesus. As interesting as this speculation is, it is only speculation. There is no reason whatsoever to think that Jesus ever saw or held any scroll from Qumran (most of which, in any event, were probably produced in Judea). Nevertheless, as we shall see in a moment, the Great Isaiah Scroll may well tell us a few things relevant to the message of Jesus and his leading disciples.

One thing we learn from the Great Isaiah Scroll and from several other scrolls from Qumran's collection is the longevity of these books. Have you ever wondered how long a book was used, before it began to fall apart and had to be discarded? So far as we know, all of the scrolls at Qumran were still in use when the community was destroyed by the Romans in either 68 or 73 CE. Approximately 40 of the scrolls, most of them Scripture scrolls, were 200 to 300 years old when the community came to an end. The books that the Greeks and Romans read were in use just as long. In fact in a recent study of libraries, collections and archives from late antiquity, George Houston found that manuscripts were in use anywhere from 150 to 500 years before being discarded.[21] It appears, so far as can be ascertained, that Christians used their manuscripts just as long. The fourth-century Codex Vaticanus (B) was re-inked in the tenth century, which shows that it was still being read and studied some 600 years after it had been produced.[22] Many other biblical codices show signs of re-inking, correcting and annotations hundreds of years after they were produced, which again testifies to their great longevity.[23]

These observations have profound implications for how we look at the preservation of the books that make up the New

Testament. If the first-century originals, or 'autographs' of the Gospels continued in use for 150 years or more, they would still have been in circulation when the oldest copies of the Gospels that we possess today were copied. Papyrus 45 from the Chester Beatty collection dates to about 220 CE. It preserves large portions of all four New Testament Gospels. It is possible, perhaps even probable that the autographs of Matthew, Mark, Luke and John were still being read and copied when Papyrus 45 was written. This means, further, that when Papyrus 45 was written the text of the Gospels was still being influenced by the autographs and the first copies of the autographs. Those who think that the autographs were lost early and that many 'generations' of copied texts lie between the autographs of the first century and our surviving early third-century copies, and that therefore the text has suffered serious distortions and alterations, must confront the evidence Houston has set forth.

The papyri, as well as the Vindolanda tablets, also show us that documents were almost always prepared in duplicate before the 'autograph' (the signed version) was sent out. Sometimes there were multiple copies made to facilitate circulation. Some of the New Testament letters appear to have been intended for circulation. These would include James, Hebrews, the Petrine letters and perhaps one or two of Paul's letters. This would mean the production of at least two copies of Matthew, two copies of Mark and so forth, before the finished product began to circulate. In effect this factor 'doubles' the chances of first-century originals surviving well into the second century and perhaps on into the third, thus overlapping with our oldest extant manuscripts.

Another benefit we derive from the examination of the ancient books, whether the Hebrew and Aramaic scrolls from Qumran or the Greek Christian Scriptures, is via study of the sigla, paragraph markers, annotations, marginal corrections and the like. Most ancient manuscripts give evidence of corrections and annotations of one sort or another. Sometimes these markings tell us something about the scribe or about how the manuscript was studied or what function it may have had in the hands of those who read it. Some manuscripts are written in tiny print and seem to be intended for private reading and perhaps easy transport, as in a 'pocket' edition.

Some are written in larger print, perhaps with paragraphing and punctuation to aid public reading.

Three of our oldest Greek New Testament manuscripts (Papyrus 45, Papyrus 66 and Papyrus 75) abbreviate the word *stauros* ('cross') by omitting the alpha and upsilon and then combining the tau and the rho letters to create what scholars call a tau-rho compendium. This compendium is a t-shaped cross with a circle at the top, thus appearing as a figure on a cross. All three of these manuscripts date to the end of the second century or beginning of the third. In combination with the late second-century Palatine Graffito, which depicts Jesus on a t-shaped cross, we have important early evidence for the configuration of the cross. In addition to that, the discussion in Justin Martyr, in his *First Apology* (*c.*155), in which he appeals to Plato's comment, 'He placed him crosswise in the universe' and suggests that it foreshadows the cross of Christ (*1 Apol.* 60.1–5), points in the same direction. Given Justin's earlier discussion of cross-shaped objects (*1 Apol.* 55: 'this shows no other form than that of the cross'), we probably have evidence here of a conscious-ness among mid second-century Christians of cross sigla, at least a generation or more before the copying of the Greek manuscripts that have been discussed.[24] It seems that the tradition of the t-shaped cross, which was believed to be the true form of the cross on which Jesus was crucified, is based on early and very probably correct information.

I conclude this section with an interesting observation of paragraph sigla in the Great Isaiah Scroll from Qumran's Cave 1. In column 43 (Figure 3.5) one can observe a prominent hat-shaped siglum in the right-hand margin, right where Isaiah 52.7 begins: 'How beautiful upon the mountains are the feet of him who brings good tidings . . . who says to Zion, "Your God reigns".' The siglum may be a combination of the Greek *paragraphos*, a long horizontal line (—) and a large samekh (the letter 's'), which indicates the beginning of a section or seder. The circle-shaped samekh resting on the horizontal line gives the siglum the appearance of a bowler hat. A simpler siglum – this time the horizontal line by itself – appears in the right-hand margin of column 44, separating 52.15 and 53.1 (Figure 3.6). (Paragraphing for the whole passage is 52.7–12, 52.13–15, 53.1–8 and 53.9–12.)

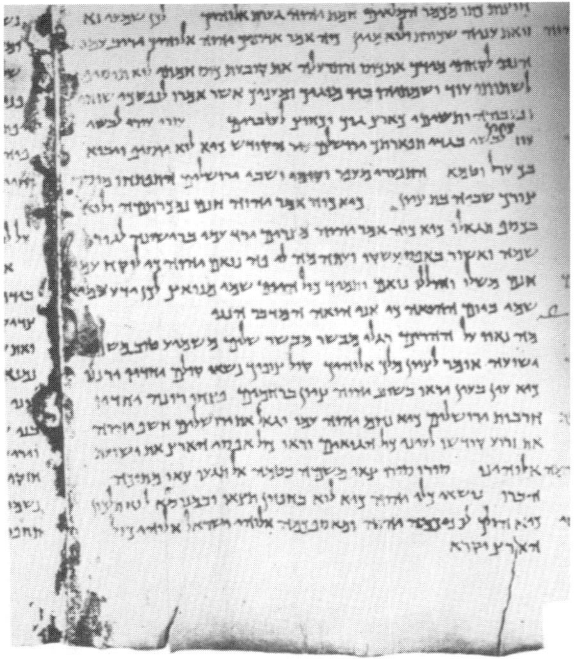

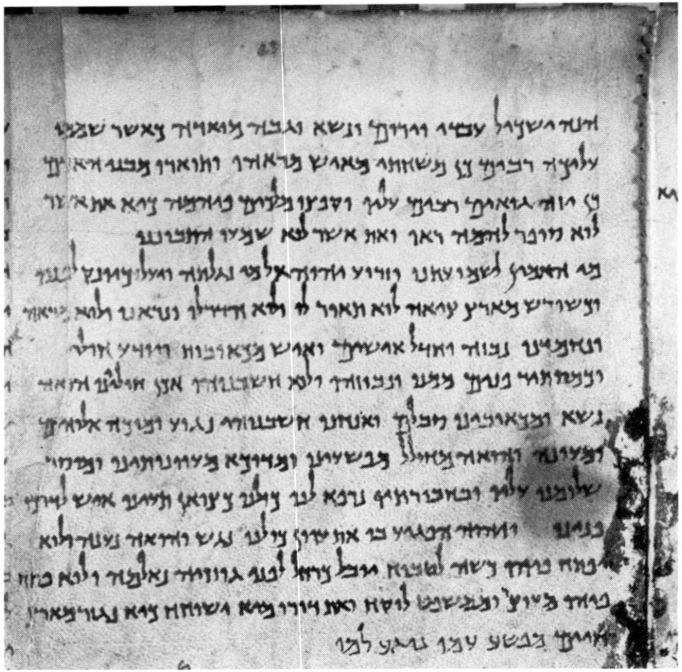

Figure 3.6 Great Isaiah Scroll, column 44
Observe the horizontal line (a Greek *paragraphos*) in the right-hand margin of column 44 (= Isa. 52.13–53.12) of the Great Isaiah Scroll. It denotes the beginning of a major subsection. Copyright © John C. Trever, PhD; digital image by James E. Trever.

Figure 3.5 Great Isaiah Scroll, column 43 (= Isaiah 52)
The Great Isaiah Scroll (1QIsaiahᵃ) dates to 100–200 BCE. Observe the 'hat'-shaped siglum in the right-hand margin. The siglum, which denotes the beginning of a major section, comprises a horizontal line (a Greek *paragraphos*), on which rests a circle (a Hebrew samekh). Copyright © John C. Trever, PhD; digital image by James E. Trever.

The sigla in the Masoretic Text, the official Hebrew version of the Old Testament on which modern translations are based, are similar though less pronounced. Accordingly, both the Great Isaiah Scroll of Qumran and the Masoretic Text appear to view Isaiah 52.7–12 and the well-known Song of the Suffering Servant, 52.13—53.12, as two related units, perhaps with 52.7–12 introducing the song. Interestingly enough, this is how several modern commentators understand the sense of Isaiah 52—53, even though no reference is made to the Great Isaiah Scroll.

Even the later Aramaic translation and paraphrase called the Targum (see Chapter 2) links Isaiah 52.7 with the Song of the Suffering Servant. We see this in a change of wording in 53.1. The Hebrew's, 'Who has believed our report?' becomes in the Targum, 'Who has believed this our good tidings?' This means that the good tidings (or gospel) announced by the prophet in 52.7 have to do with the Lord's Suffering Servant in 53.1. Indeed, the Targum goes on to identify the Servant as none other than the Messiah.

The linkage between Isaiah 52.7 and 53.1 is attested in Paul and Peter, two major figures in the early Church. Paul quotes the two passages side by side in Romans 10.15–16; they are linked allusively in Peter's speech to Cornelius (especially Acts 10.36, 43). In Christian circles the linkage of these two Isaiah passages may have originated with Jesus himself, who proclaimed: 'The kingdom of God is at hand ... believe in the gospel' (Mark 1.15). Not only does he proclaim the good tidings, or gospel, in language that derives from Isaiah 40.9 and 52.7, his language reflects the way Isaiah was being paraphrased and interpreted in Aramaic in the synagogue. In the Targum the good tidings of these passages are summed up in the words, 'The kingdom of your God is revealed!' Yet Jesus will later tell his disciples, in language that echoes the Song of the Suffering Servant, that 'the Son of man also came not to be served but to serve, and to give his life as a ransom for many' (Mark 10.45; Isa. 53.8, 10, 12). Indeed, in John's Gospel Jesus declares that the Son of Man must be 'lifted up' (John 12.31, 34). In saying this he alludes to Isaiah 52.13: 'Behold, my servant ... shall be lifted up, and shall be very high.' A few verses later the Johannine evangelist quotes Isaiah 53.1: 'Who has believed our report?' (John 12.38), thus strengthening the link between Jesus the Son of Man and the Suffering Servant of Isaiah 52.13—53.12.

But did Jesus know the Scriptures of his people? In the Gospels he quotes or alludes to the sacred Scriptures many times. Is this the authentic Jesus or later glossing of the story? Could Jesus read the Scriptures? To this important question we now turn.

Could Jesus read?

Three passages in the Gospels suggest that Jesus was able to read. The first is Luke 4.16–30, which describes Jesus reading from the scroll of Isaiah and then preaching a homily. Most scholars hesitate to draw firm conclusions from this passage because of its relationship to the parallel passage in Mark 6.1–6, which says nothing about reading Scripture. The second passage is John 8.6, which says Jesus stooped down and wrote in the dust with his finger. The problem here is that in all probability this passage (John 7.53—8.11) is inauthentic. Even if the passage is accepted as preserving a genuine reminiscence of something Jesus did, it tells us nothing certain about Jesus' literacy. He may have been doing nothing more than doodling.

The third passage, John 7.15, directly speaks to the question of Jesus' literacy, at least in the narrative world of the fourth evangelist. Some in Jerusalem wonder: 'How is it that this man has learning, when he has never studied?' Literally, they have asked how he 'knows letters' (*grammata oiden*), 'not having studied' or 'not having learned' (*mē memathēkōs*). But the reference here is to a lack of formal, scribal training, not to having had no education whatsoever. The question was raised because Jesus has not sat at the feet of a trained, recognized rabbi or sage. We encounter the same language in the book of Acts, which describes the reaction of the religious authorities to the disciples of Jesus: 'Now when they saw the boldness of Peter and John, and perceived that they were uneducated [*agrammatoi*], common men [*idiōtai*], they wondered; and they recognized that they had been with Jesus' (Acts 4.13). The words *agrammatoi* and *idiōtai* should not be rendered 'unlearned and ignorant', as in the King James Version and ASV. To be *agrammatos* (the singular form of the adjective) is to lack scribal training (so Liddell, Scott and Jones, *Greek–English Lexicon*), and is in fact the opposite of the *grammateus*, the professional 'scribe'. To be *agrammatos* does not necessarily mean to be unable to read.

To be an *idiōtēs* (the singular of *idiōtai*) is to be one outside of the guild or outside of the group, as in 1 Corinthians 14.16, 23 and 24, where Paul refers to the 'outsider' (so RSV) or 'ungifted' (so NASB) as an *idiōtēs*. In contrast to professional, trained scribes and priests, the *idiōtēs* is a layman. In 2 Corinthians 11.6, Paul says of himself, 'Even if I am unskilled [*idiōtēs*] in speaking' (RSV). Paul, of course, could and did preach, and did so effectively. Yet he conceded that he lacked formal training in rhetoric and oratory. Hence he regarded himself as 'unskilled' or outside the guild. *Idiōtēs* may also refer to a commoner, in contrast to royalty. The *idiōtēs* is the unskilled (with reference to any profession or trade) or commoner (in contrast to a ruler), and seems to be the equivalent of the Hebrew *hediyot*, as seen in the Mishnah, the early third-century compilation of Jewish law: 'He that is not skilled [*hahediyot*] may sew after his usual fashion, but the craftsman may make only irregular stitches' (*m. Mo'ed Qat.* 1.8); 'Three kings and four commoners [*hediyototh*] have no share in the world to come' (*m. Sanh.* 10.2).

The comments in John 7.15 and Acts 4.13 should not be taken to imply that Jesus and his disciples were illiterate. In fact the opposite is probably the intended sense, as most commentators rightly interpret. That is, despite not having had formal training, Jesus and his disciples evince remarkable skill in the knowledge of Scripture and ability to interpret it and defend their views. These texts, more than Luke 4.16–30 and John 8.6, lend some support to the probability that Jesus was literate.

One might also mention the *titulus*, which announces the reason for the execution, placed on or near Jesus' cross: 'The king of the Jews' (Mark 15.26; Matt. 27.37; Luke 23.37). Its placement surely implies that some people observing Jesus could read, among them perhaps his own disciples, for whom the *titulus* serves as a warning, in keeping with Roman policy of public execution as a deterrence. According to the fourth Gospel: 'Many of the Jews read this title, for the place where Jesus was crucified was near the city; and it was written in Hebrew, in Latin, and in Greek' (John 19.20). It is interesting to note that the evangelist could assume that 'many' Judeans were able to read the *titulus*.

Although there is no unambiguous evidence for the literacy of Jesus, there is considerable contextual and circumstantial evidence that suggests that in all probability he was literate. At the outset we should keep in mind the nature of Jewish faith itself. It is centred on Scripture, which narrates Israel's sacred story, a story that the Jewish people are admonished to know and to teach their children. According to the Shema, which all Torah-observant Jews were expected to recite daily, parents were to teach their children Torah (Deut. 4.9; 6.7; 11.19; 31.12–13; 2 Chron. 17.7–9; Eccles. 12.9), even to adorn their doorposts with the Shema (Deut. 6.9: 'you shall write [Hebrew: *ketavka*; Greek: *grapsete*] them on the doorposts of your house and on your gates'; see also 11.20). One should suppose that scriptural commandments such as these, which stand at the heart of Jewish faith (Mark 12.28–33; Jas. 2.19), would have encouraged literacy among the Jewish people.

According to Philo and Josephus, approximate contemporaries of Jesus, Jewish parents taught their children Torah and how to read it. Philo claims: 'All men guard their own customs, but this is especially true of the Jewish nation. Holding that the laws are oracles vouchsafed by God and having been trained [*paideuthentes*] in this doctrine from their earliest years, they carry the likenesses of the commandments enshrined in their souls' (*Embassy* 210). It is improbable that the training of which he speaks here did not include basic literacy. Josephus, however, is more explicit: 'Above all we pride ourselves on the education of our children [*paidotrophian*], and regard as the most essential task in life the observance of our laws and of the pious practices, based thereupon, which we have inherited' (*Ag. Ap.* 1.60). He says later: '(The law) orders that (children) shall be taught to read [*grammata paideuein*], and shall learn both the laws and the deeds of their forefathers' (*Ag. Ap.* 2.204).

The claim that the law 'orders' children to be taught to read derives from Deuteronomy 6.9 and 11.20 (cited above). Josephus goes so far as to say that:

> most men, so far from living in accordance with their own laws, hardly know what they are . . . But, should anyone of our nation be questioned about the laws, he would repeat them all more readily than his own name. The result, then, of our thorough grounding in

> the laws from the first dawn of intelligence is that we have them, as
> it were, engraven on our souls. (*Ag. Ap.* 2.176, 178)

This may not be too wide of the truth, for Augustine claims that
Seneca made a similar remark: 'The Jews, however, are aware of the
origin and meaning of their rites. The greater part of (other) people
go through a ritual not knowing why they do so' (*The City of God*
6.11).

It may be admitted that Philo and Josephus are painting idealistic
pictures and perhaps have in mind affluent families that can afford
the luxury of formal education for their children. But it would be a
mistake to assume that the pursuit of education, including above all
literacy, was limited to the upper class or to professionals. In the
story of the seven martyred sons (2 Macc. 7) we have no reason to
imagine an upper-class family. In the version presented in 4 Maccabees
the mother reminds her sons of their father's teaching:

> He, while he was still with you, taught you the Law and the Prophets.
> He read to you of Abel, slain by Cain, of Isaac, offered as a burnt
> offering, and of Joseph, in prison. He spoke to you of the zeal of
> Phineas, taught you about Hananiah ... He reminded you of the
> scripture of Isaiah which says ... [Isa. 43.2] ... He sang to you the
> psalm of David which says ... [Ps. 34.19] ... He recited the proverb
> of Solomon which says ... [Prov. 3.18] ... He affirmed the word of
> Ezekiel [Ezek. 37.3] ... Nor did he forget the song that Moses taught
> which says ... [Deut. 32.39]. (4 Macc. 18.10–19)

The summary here of the father's instruction of his sons clearly
presupposes literacy. The portrait is idealized to be sure, but for it
to have any persuasive value in Jewish society it would have to be
at least somewhat realistic.

Popular piety expressed in the earliest rabbinic tradition coheres
with the testimonies of Philo and Josephus. The sages enjoin, 'provide
yourself a teacher' (*'Abot* 1.16; 1.6). In the saying attributed to Judah
ben Tema, literacy is assumed to be the norm: 'At five years old [one
is fit] for the Scripture, at ten for the Mishnah, at thirteen for [keep-
ing] the commandments (that is, *bar mitsvah*)' (*'Abot* 5.21; *b. Ketub.*
50a: 'Do not accept a pupil under the age of six; but accept one from
the age of six and stuff him [with knowledge] like an ox'). Elsewhere
in the Mishnah we read that 'children ... should be educated ... so

that they will be familiar with the commandments' (*m. Yoma* 8.4). We find a similar injunction in the Tannaitic midrash on Deuteronomy: 'Once an infant begins to talk, his father should converse with him in the holy tongue and should teach him Torah, for if he fails to do so it is the same as if he had buried him' (*Sipre Deut.* §56 (on Deut. 11.19); *t. Qidd.* 1.11: 'What is the father's duty towards his son? . . . to teach him Torah'). If a son lacks the intelligence to ask his father the proper questions concerning the meaning of Passover, his father is to instruct him (*m. Pesah.* 10.4). There is legal discussion that clearly presupposes that children can read Scripture (*m. Meg.* 4.5–6; *t. Šabb.* 11.17: 'If a minor holds the pen'; *Soperim* 5.9: regulations concerning producing extracts of Scripture for children). One of the first things a new proselyte is to learn is the Hebrew alphabet, forwards and backwards (*b. Šabb.* 31a, in reference to Hillel). The rabbinic tradition contains numerous references to schools, to the effect that every synagogue and village had at least one school. The idealistic and tendentious nature of this material is often not adequately appreciated. Primarily on the basis of the rabbinic tradition, Shemuel Safrai concludes that 'the ability to write was fairly widespread . . . [but] less widespread than that of reading which everyone possessed'.[25] Notwithstanding his uncritical use of rabbinical sources,[26] Safrai's conclusion that literacy was widespread among Jews may be more correct than not.

Recognizing the limited value of the late, idealized rabbinic literature and the apologetically oriented claims of Philo and Josephus, three general factors favour the probability of the literacy of Jesus. First, the injunctions of Scripture to teach and learn Torah; second, the value placed on Torah, of knowing and obeying its laws; and third, the advantage of being the first-born son. In view of these factors it is probable that Jesus received at least some education in literacy.[27] The probability increases when we take into account features of his later ministry. In these we have, I believe, far more compelling evidence for the literacy of Jesus.

Jesus is frequently called 'Rabbi' (Mark 9.5; 11.21; 14.45; etc.), 'Rabbo(u)ni' (Mark 10.51; John 20.16) or its Greek equivalents, 'master' (*epistata*; Luke 5.5; 8.24, 45; 9.33, 49; 17.13) or 'teacher' (*didaskalos*; Matt. 8.19; 9.11; 12.38; Mark 4.38; 5.35; 9.17; 10.17, 20; 12.14, 19, 32; Luke 19.39; John 1.38; 3.2). Jesus refers to himself in this manner and is called such by supporters, opponents and non-partisans. Although prior to 70 CE the designation 'Rabbi' is informal, even vague, and lacks the later connotations of formal training and ordination (which obtain some time after the destruction of Jerusalem and the temple),[28] it is very probable that at least a limited literacy was assumed.

In keeping with his designation as Rabbi, Jesus and others called his closest followers 'disciples', whose Greek form (*mathētai*; Mark 2.15, 16, 18, 23; 3.7, 9; 4.34; 5.31; and Q: Luke 6.20; 10.23; 12.22; 14.26, 27), like the Hebrew (*talmidim*; *'Abot* 1.1, 11; 2.8; 5.12; 6.6), derives from the verbal cognate 'to learn' (*manthanein/lamad*). 'This, in turn, is education [*paideia*] in the law, by which we learn [*manthanomen*] divine matters reverently and human affairs to our advantage' (4 Macc. 1.17). This terminology, whose appearance in the Gospels betrays no hint that it was controversial or in any sense a matter of debate, or the product of early Christian tendentiousness, creates a strong presumption in favour of Jesus' literacy. In the Jewish setting, an *illiterate* rabbi who surrounds himself with disciples, and debates Scripture and legal matters with other rabbis and scribes, is hardly credible. Moreover the numerous parallels between Jesus' teaching and the rabbinic tradition, as well as the many points of agreement between his interpretation of Scripture and the rabbinic tradition,[29] only add to this conviction. Jesus' teaching in the synagogues (Matt. 4.23; 9.35; Mark 1.21; 6.2; Luke 4.15; 6.6; 13.10; John 6.59) is not easily explained if Jesus were unable to read and had not undertaken study of Scripture that involved at least some training in literacy.

In the style of the sages and rabbis of his day, Jesus 'sat down' when he taught (Matt. 5.1; 26.55; Mark 12.41; Luke 4.20; 5.3; see also the rabbinic discussion of when to sit or stand in *b. Meg.* 21a). Jesus himself refers to the scribes and Pharisees who 'sit on the seat of Moses' (Matt. 23.2). Moreover Jesus' contemporaries compared him with scribes; that is, with literate people: 'And they were astonished at his teaching, for he taught them as one who had authority, and not as the scribes' (Mark 1.22). Although such comparison in itself does not prove that Jesus was literate, it supports the Gospels' portrait that Jesus was a rabbi or teacher, which in turn should require a presumption in favour of literacy. It is difficult to imagine

Jesus enjoying a favourable comparison with rival scribes if – unlike them – he was illiterate.

On occasion Jesus himself refers to reading Scripture. He asks Pharisees who criticized his disciples for plucking grain on the sabbath: 'Have you never read what David did, when he was in need and was hungry . . .?' (Mark 2.25; Matt. 12.3). To this pericope Matthew adds: 'Or have you not read in the law how on the Sabbath the priests in the temple profane the Sabbath, and are guiltless?' (Matt. 12.5; 19.4 – where Matthew again enriches the Markan source in a similar manner; the same is probably the case in Matt. 21.16). In another polemical context, Jesus asks the ruling priests and elders: 'Have you not read this scripture: "The very stone which the builders rejected has become the head of the corner . . ."?' (Mark 12.10). Later he asks the Sadducees, who had raised a question about resurrection: 'And as for the dead being raised, have you not read in the book of Moses, in the passage about the bush, how God said to him, "I am the God of Abraham, and the God of Isaac, and the God of Jacob"?' (Mark 12.26). In a discussion with a legal expert who has asked what one must do to inherit eternal life, Jesus asks in turn: 'What is written in the Law? How do you read?' (Luke 10.26). We find in the rabbinic literature phrasing such as 'Similarly you read' (for example *b. Šabb.* 97a; *b. Ketub.* 111a, 111b) or 'How would you read this verse?' (for example *b. Ketub.* 81b; *b. Qidd.* 22a, 40a, 81b). But Jesus' rhetorical and pointed 'Have you not read?' seems to be distinctive of his style and surely would have little argumentative force if he himself could not read.[30] And finally, even if we discount Luke 4.16–30 as the evangelist's retelling of Mark 6.1–6, it may nevertheless accurately recall Jesus' habit of reading and expounding Scripture in the synagogues of Galilee: 'And he came to Nazareth, where he had been brought up; and he went to the synagogue, *as his custom was*, on the Sabbath day. And he stood up to read' (Luke 4.16; emphasis added). I shall return to this passage below.

It should be noted too that in the Gospel stories reviewed above, Jesus' literacy is never an issue. There is no evidence of apologetic tendencies on the part of the evangelists, in which Jesus' literary skills are exaggerated, or any sense that Jesus' literary skills are in some way deficient. Jesus' ability to read appears to be a given, not an issue.

Indications of Jesus' literacy may also be seen in his familiarity with and usage of Scripture. According to the Synoptic Gospels, Jesus quotes or alludes to 23 of the 36 books of the Hebrew Bible[31] (counting the books of Samuel, Kings and Chronicles as three books, not six). Jesus alludes to or quotes all five books of Moses, the three Major Prophets (Isaiah, Jeremiah and Ezekiel), eight of the twelve Minor Prophets (Hosea, Joel, Amos, Jonah, Micah, Zephaniah, Zechariah and Malachi; omitted are Obadiah, Nahum, Habakkuk and Haggai) and five of the 'writings' (Psalms, Proverbs, Job, Daniel and Chronicles. Omitted are Song of Solomon, Ruth, Lamentations, Ecclesiastes, Esther, Ezra and Nehemiah). In other words, Jesus quotes or alludes to *all* of the books of the law, *most* of the Prophets and *some* of the Writings. According to the Synoptic Gospels, Jesus quotes or alludes to Deuteronomy some 15 or 16 times, Isaiah some 40 times and the Psalms some 13 times. These appear to be his favourite books, though Daniel and Zechariah seem to have been favourites also. Superficially, then, the 'canon' of Jesus is pretty much what it was for most religiously observant Jews of his time,[32] including – and especially – the producers of the scrolls at Qumran.[33] Moreover there is evidence that villages and synagogues in the time

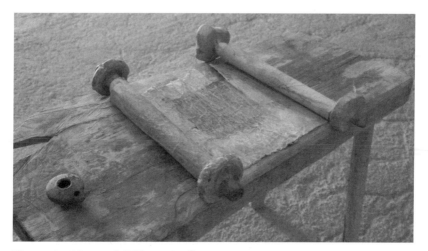

Figure 3.7 Nazareth Village scroll
Scroll and reading table replicas at the Nazareth Village. Photograph courtesy of Ginny Evans.

of Jesus did in fact possess biblical scrolls (1 Macc. 1.56–57; Josephus, *J.W.* 2.229 (in reference to Antiochus IV's efforts to find and destroy Torah scrolls); *Life* 134 (in reference to scrolls in Galilee, during the early stages of the revolt against Rome))).

Finally, the frequency and poignancy of Jesus' employment of Aramaic tradition in his allusions and interpretations of Scripture are suggestive of literacy, regular participation in the synagogue (where the Aramaic paraphrase, or Targum, developed) and acquaintance with rabbinic and scribal education itself.[34] The dictional, thematic and exegetical coherence between the teachings of Jesus and the emerging Aramaic tradition has been well documented and need not be rehearsed here.

The data that have been surveyed are more easily explained in reference to a literate Jesus, a Jesus who could read the Hebrew Scriptures, could paraphrase and interpret them in Aramaic and could do so in a manner that indicated his familiarity with current interpretive tendencies in both popular circles (as in the synagogues) and in professional, even elite circles (as seen in debates with scribes, ruling priests and elders). Of course, to conclude that Jesus was literate is not necessarily to conclude that Jesus had received formal scribal training. The data do not suggest this. Jesus' innovative, experiential approach to Scripture and to Jewish faith seems to suggest the contrary.

I find an illiterate Jesus harder to explain than a literate one. Jesus was regarded as a teacher – by friend and foe alike. He argued points of Scripture with scribes, Pharisees, Sadducees and ruling priests. He specifically challenged their readings of Scripture. He taught disciples – 'learners' – who in turn preserved his teaching. The movement that Jesus founded produced a legacy of literature, including four Gospels, a narrative of the early Church (Acts) and a number of letters. The sudden emergence of a prolific literary tradition from an illiterate founder is not impossible of course, but it is less difficult to explain if Jesus were in fact literate.

4

Confronting the establishment:
ruling priests and the temple

When Jesus and his following entered Jerusalem one week before Passover, confrontations with ruling priests and their colleagues began almost immediately. When he entered the sacred precincts, in which were located the sanctuary and a number of supporting buildings, Jesus 'began to drive out those who sold and those who bought in the temple, and he overturned the tables of the money-changers and the seats of those who sold pigeons; and he would not allow anyone to carry anything through the temple' (Mark 11.15–16). But the most daring thing that Jesus did was to condemn the temple authorities: 'Is it not written, "My house shall be called a house of prayer for all the nations"? But you have made it a "den of robbers"' (Mark 11.17). The first quotation is from Isaiah 56.7, part of an oracle that recalls Solomon's prayer of dedication concerning the completed temple (1 Kings 8.43). The second is from Jeremiah 7.11, part of a passage recounting Jeremiah's angry confrontation with the ruling priests of his day. The point that Jesus has made is that not only has the temple establishment of his day failed to live up to Solomon's prayer and Isaiah's vision that the temple become a house of prayer for all people, it has in fact become a place of crime. The allusion to Jeremiah 7 is especially disturbing because the prophet goes on to warn the ruling priests of impending destruction.

The conflict between Jesus and the ruling priests escalates. The priests demand to know by what authority Jesus has acted. He counters by demanding that the priests state their position with regard to the popular and recently martyred John the Baptist (Mark 11.27–33). Although the priests refuse to answer, Jesus answers in an indirect way the question put to him by telling the parable of the Vineyard Tenants (Mark 12.1–11), a parable based on Isaiah's song of the well-cared-for but ultimately fruitless vineyard (Isa. 5.1–7). The priests rightly recognize that Jesus had told the parable 'against them' (Mark 12.12), for they know that Isaiah's Song of the Vineyard had become understood as directed specifically against the temple establishment and not the people in general.

At one time evidence for this interpretation was limited to the Targum of Isaiah, which in 5.1–7 spoke of the temple and altar instead of watchtower and wine vat (as in the Hebrew text), an exegesis repeated in rabbinic tradition (*t. Meʿila* 1.16 and *t. Sukkah* 3.15). The antiquity of this cultic interpretation is now partially attested by 4Q500, whose fragmentary lines 3–7 read: 'a wine vat [bu]ilt among stones . . . to the gate of the holy height . . . your planting and the streams of your glory . . . your vine[yard]'. Holy 'height' agrees with the Aramaic's description of the fertile hill as 'high', while the 'streams' agrees with *t. Sukkah*'s water channels. Of course, the reference to the height as 'holy' is an obvious allusion to the Temple Mount (Ezek. 20.40: 'For on my holy mountain, the mountain height of Israel, says the Lord God, there all the house of Israel, all of them, shall serve me in the land'). Jesus' use of Isaiah 5.1–7 presupposes several of the principal exegetical points of reference preserved in 4Q500, a text that predates him, and in the Targum and Tosefta, texts that postdate him.[1]

The discovery of a scroll fragment explains the exegetical cut and thrust. An archaeological discovery enables us to appreciate more fully the sensitivities with respect to the temple's holiness. Jesus' threatening prophetic indictment of the ruling priests was bad enough, but the implied threat against the temple itself was even more offensive. I say this because the purity and sanctity of the temple precincts, especially the sanctuary itself, were closely guarded. The public, moreover, was given notice in language hard not to understand.

In 1871 Charles Clermont-Ganneau found a limestone block, about 85 cm long, 57 cm high and 37 cm thick, on which was inscribed a warning to Gentiles to stay out of the perimeter surrounding the sanctuary (Figure 4.1). The inscription reads as follows (*OGIS* no. 598; *CIJ* no. 1400; *SEG* VIII 169):

Let no Gentile enter
within the partition and barrier
surrounding the temple; whosoever
is caught shall be responsible
for his subsequent
death.

A fragment of a second inscription was found in 1935 outside the wall around Jerusalem's Old City. This is 50 cm high, 31 cm thick and about 25 cm wide (the width varies due to the jagged right-hand edge). The inscribed letters were originally painted red, making them stand out against the off-white limestone. The extant text of the fragmentary inscription matches closely the wording and layout of the fully preserved inscription.[2]

Figure 4.1 Temple Warning
The famous 'Temple Warning', inscribed in stone, threatens with death any Gentile who gets too close to the Jerusalem temple. The inscription is housed in Istanbul. Photograph courtesy of www.HolyLandPhotographs.org.

This inscription is almost certainly one of the inscribed warnings mentioned by Josephus. For example, he states: 'Upon [the partition wall of the temple court] stood pillars, at equal distances from one another, declaring the law of purity, some in Greek, and some in Roman letters, that "no foreigner should go within that holy place"' (*J.W.* 5.193–94; see also 6.124–28; *Ant.* 15.417; *Ag. Ap.* 2.103). Philo refers to the same law and penalty, though without mention of the inscribed warnings: 'Still more abounding and peculiar is the zeal of them all for the temple, and the strongest proof of this is that death without appeal is the sentence against those of other races who penetrate into its inner confines' (*Embassy* 212). Allusions to the death penalty for temple violations are found also in the later rabbinic literature (for example *Sipre Num.* §116 (on Num. 18.1–32): 'Rabbi Joshua ben Hananiah sought to help Rabbi Yohanan ben Gudegedah [at the gates of the temple. But] he said to him, "Go back, for you have already have risked your life, since I belong to the gatekeepers, but you are a singer"').

The scriptural backdrop for these posted warnings includes 1 Kings 8.41–43, which recounts Solomon's prayer of dedication, in which it is anticipated that Gentiles will visit the temple, Numbers 1.51, which warns, 'If anyone else comes near [the tabernacle], he shall be put to death' (Num. 3.38; 19.13; Lev. 10.2; 15.31; 22.9), and Leviticus 16.2, where Moses is warned by God, 'Tell Aaron your brother not to come at all times into the holy place within the veil, before the mercy seat which is upon the ark, lest he die.' Thus there was the expectation, on the one hand, that Gentiles may approach the temple, but there were restrictions, with deadly consequences, on the other. Subsequent interpretation, custom and tradition established the guidelines that were observed late in the Second Temple period. Partitions and warnings against trespass by non-members or the uninitiated were common in late antiquity and were observed by non-Jews, as well as Jews.

The inscription discovered by Clermont-Ganneau corroborates, to be sure, an important Second Temple detail recounted in Philo and Josephus. But from a Christian perspective the primary value of this inscription is its contribution to a better understanding of the setting and context of Jesus' action in the temple precincts and of the riot that overtook Paul in the same precincts some years later

(Acts 21.27–36, especially v. 28, where the accusation is levelled against Paul that 'he also brought Greeks into the temple, and he has defiled this holy place'). It is in the light of this highly sensitive appreciation of the temple precincts, especially that of the carefully protected sanctuary within them, that Jesus' remarks should be understood.

Archaeological discovery sheds light on yet another aspect of Jesus' controversy with the temple establishment. A papyrus fragment reads:

> And taking along the disciples he entered the holy court and was walking about in the temple. And approaching, a certain Pharisee, a ruling priest, whose name was Levi, met them and said to the Saviour, 'Who permitted you to walk in this place of purification and to see these holy vessels, when you have not washed nor yet have your disciples bathed their feet? But defiled you have walked in this Temple, which is a pure place, in which no other person walks unless he has washed himself and changed his clothes, neither does he dare view these holy vessels.' And the Saviour immediately stood [still] with his disciples and answered him, 'Are you then, being here in the Temple, clean?' He says to him, 'I am clean, for I washed in the pool of David, and having descended by one set of steps I ascended by another. And I put on white and clean clothes, and then I came and looked upon these holy vessels.' Answering, the Saviour said to him, 'Woe you blind who do not see. You have washed in these running waters in which dogs and swine have been cast night and day, and have cleaned and wiped the outside skin, which also the harlots and flute-girls anoint and wash and wipe and beautify for the lust of men; but within they are full of scorpions and all wickedness. But I and my disciples, who you say have not bathed, have been dipped in the waters of eternal life which come from . . . But woe to the . . .'
>
> (P. Oxy. 840, with restorations)

This interesting story is not found in the Gospels but is preserved on a tiny piece of papyrus that was part of a very small book or perhaps had been a text rolled up in an amulet. Although the story depicts the temple setting realistically, most scholars regard it as apocryphal. The reference to the temple as 'this place of purification' coheres with the warning inscriptions already discussed. The debate over purification, raised by a ruling priest who happens to be a

Pharisee, is consistent with the debate between Jesus and Pharisees over purity and food (Mark 7.1–23).

The reference to seeing 'holy vessels' may well reflect a custom in which the holy temple utensils on occasion were put on display.[3] The priest's assertion, 'having descended by one set of steps I ascended by another', has been shown to reflect quite accurately the design and function of the *miqva'ot* (purification pools) that have been uncovered in the immediate vicinity of the Temple Mount. In some of these stepped pools one can observe dividers that run down the middle of the steps, thus indicating that people went down on one side of the steps and came up on the other (Figure 4.2). We see this also at Qumran, in a very large *miqveh*[4] (Figure 4.3).

Our apocryphal story also presupposes the elitism and arrogance of a ruling priesthood that looks with contempt on the ordinary folk. The author of the pseudepigraphal *Testament of Moses*, which is dated to about 30 CE, gives colourful expression to this arrogance:

> They consume the goods of the (poor), saying their acts are according to justice, (while in fact they are simply) exterminators, deceitfully seeking to conceal themselves so that they will not be known as completely godless because of their criminal deeds (committed) all the day long, saying, 'We shall have feasts, even luxurious winings and dinings. Indeed, we shall behave ourselves as princes.' They, with hand and mind, touch impure things, yet their mouths will speak enormous things, and they will even say, 'Do not touch me, lest you pollute me in the position I occupy.' (*T. Mos.* 7.6–10)

The desire not to be touched lest one is polluted may be reflected in the parable of the Good Samaritan, in which the priest and Levite do not stop to assist the wounded man but pass by 'on the other side' of the road (Luke 10.31–32). One also thinks of the contrast seen in Jesus, who touches people, even lepers and the dead (for example Mark 1.41; 5.41; 7.33; 8.22; Luke 7.14). The story recounted in P. Oxy. 840 may be apocryphal but it authentically reflects the world of Jesus and the temple establishment of his day. One might say that the story reflects authentic context even if the story as told never happened.

The Synoptic Gospels tell us that when Jesus was arrested he was taken to the house of Caiaphas the high priest (so Matthew

Figure 4.2 *Miqveh*, Jerusalem
Not far from the southwest corner of Jerusalem's Temple Mount, this *miqveh* (from the bottom looking up) has divided steps, separating the descending impure from the ascending pure. Photograph courtesy of Anders Runesson.

Figure 4.3 *Miqveh*, Qumran
This plastered, stepped immersion pool was damaged by an earthquake in 31 BCE. Again, note the two dividers that run up and down the middle of the steps, separating the ritually pure who ascend from the water from the ritually impure who descend into the water.

explicitly; Mark and Luke implicitly). John tells us that Jesus was taken to the house of Annas, the father-in-law of Caiaphas. Archaeological excavations may have located the house of Caiaphas and the tombs of the families of Annas and Caiaphas. At least one archaeologist thinks that Annas and Caiaphas shared the same house, located in the Upper City not far from the palaces of Agrippa and Berenice (Josephus, *J.W.* 2.427). Various houses belonging to the wealthy have been excavated in this area, revealing stepped *miqva'ot*, floors with mosaic tiles, plastered and painted walls – in some cases displaying outstanding artistic talent – and the broken remains of ceramic and stoneware (Figure 4.4). The presence of stoneware is important for it testifies to the Jewish concerns with ritual purity, as we saw in Chapter 1.[5]

Not only do the ruins of the aristocratic homes testify to the wealth of the ruling priests and their peers; so do the ruins of their tombs.

Figure 4.4 Priestly mansion, Jerusalem
A partly restored room in a mansion destroyed in 70 CE, excavated in the Jewish Quarter of Old Jerusalem, thought to have belonged to a high priest. In contrast to pagan art, the floor mosaic presents no human figures or mythological themes. The stone vessels are indicative of Jewish purity laws.

At Akeldama the lower portion of a tomb complex has been excavated that may have belonged to the family of Annas, high priest from 6–15 CE.[6] The remains of this tomb suggest that in its pristine condition the tomb would have been very impressive, not unlike the beautiful monumental tombs that adorn the Kidron Valley at the foot of the Mount of Olives.

Annas (or Ananus) the high priest, whose five sons and son-in-law Caiaphas served terms as high priest (Josephus, *Ant.* 20.198), is mentioned in the New Testament (Luke 3.2: 'the high-priesthood of Annas and Caiaphas'; John 18.13: 'they led him to Annas; for he was the father-in-law of Caiaphas'; Acts 4.6: 'Annas the high priest and Caiaphas and John and Alexander, and all who were of high-priestly family'). According to Josephus, the father of Annas is one Sethi (*Ant.* 18.26). This is probably the priestly family excoriated in rabbinic tradition (*b. Pesahim* 57a; *m. Keritot* 1.7). (For more on the tombs in and around Jerusalem, see Chapter 5.)

The most intriguing discovery may relate to the son-in-law of Annas, the high priest Caiaphas who condemned Jesus and handed him over to the Roman governor. In November 1990, while working in Jerusalem's Peace Forest (North Talpiyot), which is 1.5 km south of the Old City, a crew inadvertently uncovered a crypt with four loculi in which twelve ossuaries were discovered. Happily, most of the ossuaries were found intact, unmolested by grave robbers. Coins and the style of writing seen in the inscriptions have dated these ossuaries to the first century CE. On one of the ornate ossuaries (no. 6, measuring 74 cm in length, 29 cm in width and 38 cm in height; now on display in the Israel Museum in Jerusalem), two very interesting inscriptions were found (Figure 4.5). The inscriptions have been transcribed as follows:[7]

Yehoseph bar
Qyph'

Yehoseph bar Qph'

Translated:

Joseph son of
Qayafa

Joseph son of Qafa

This ossuary contained the bones of a 60-year-old man (and those of two infants, a toddler, a young boy and a woman), and is thought by some, including the authorities of the aforementioned museum, to be the ossuary of Caiaphas the high priest, to whom Josephus refers as Joseph Caiaphas (*Ant.* 18.35: 'Joseph who is Caiaphas' and 18.95: 'the high priest Joseph called Caiaphas') and the Gospels and Acts call more simply 'Caiaphas' (Matt. 26.3, 57; Luke 3.2; John 11.49; 18.13, 14, 24, 28; Acts 4.6). Those who think the ossuary belonged to Caiaphas vocalize the inscribed name as *Qayapha* (or *Qayyapha*), the Hebrew or Aramaic equivalent of the Greek Caiaphas.

A second ossuary in the tomb (no. 3) bears the name *qf'* (vowels to come later!). In a third ossuary (no. 8), containing the bones of a woman and bearing the name *miryam berat shim'on* ('Miriam, daughter of Simon'), a coin minted during the reign of Herod Agrippa I (42/43 CE, with inscription *basleos* [*agrippa*] 'King [Agrippa]') was found in the mouth of the skull, probably reflecting the pagan custom of payment to the Greek god Charon for safe

Figure 4.5 Caiaphas ossuary
An ornate ossuary thought to have contained the skeletal remains of the high priest Caiaphas and a number of his relatives. On the end, the words *Yosef bar Qapha* can be seen.

passage across the River Styx, a custom documented as early as the fifth century BCE and perhaps implying belief in an afterlife.[8] Knowledge among Jewish priestly aristocrats of Greek afterlife mythology is attested by Josephus (*J.W.* 2.155–56), by at least one epitaph (*IG* no. 1648: 'O pitiless Charon') and by later rabbinic tradition (*b. Mo'ed Qat.* 28b, in a lament for the departed: 'tumbling aboard the ferry and having to borrow his fare'). Depictions of boats on Jewish ossuaries or crypt walls may also allude to the belief of the deceased ferried across the water to the land of the dead.[9] Saul Lieberman thinks that the 'numerous boats on the Jewish graves in Palestine most probably represent the ferry to the other world, i.e. either the divine bark of the ancient Orientals, or Charon's ferry of the Greeks'.[10] Benjamin Mazar, however, thinks boat drawings depict only transport of the coffin or ossuary from overseas to the Holy Land.[11] But Lieberman's explanation is more plausible; after all, overland modes of transport (horses, carts, wagons and the like) are not depicted in burial settings.

Several scholars and archaeologists have concluded that the Joseph bar Qyph' ossuary belonged to the former high priest, 'Joseph called Qayapha' (as Josephus refers to him). Indeed, some regard the identification as a foregone conclusion, as seen, for example, in the confidence expressed by Dominic Crossan and Jonathan Reed: 'There should be no doubt that the chamber was the resting place of the family of the high priest Caiaphas named in the gospels for his role in the crucifixion, and it's very likely that the elderly man's bones were those of Caiaphas himself.'[12] Nevertheless, there is reason for doubt.

Some scholars, including Emile Puech and William Horbury, have expressed reservations.[13] They cite three principal reasons for doubting the high priestly identification. The first lies in the fact that the crypt in which the ossuary was found is not on the level of ostentation that one would have expected to find in the case of a former high priest and son-in-law of Annas, the most influential high priest of the first century. In contrast to the ornate, almost palatial crypt of Annas described above, the 'Caiaphas' crypt is relatively plain. Respected archaeologist Shimon Gibson is not troubled by this argument. The 'basement' portions of tombs, which are often all that has survived from antiquity, are not certain indicators of the quality of the superstructure that once stood. Gibson has a good point.[14]

A second reason for doubting the Caiaphas identification lies in the spelling of the name. It is not at all clear that the second letter in *qyf* is a *yod*; it may well be a *waw*, that is, *qwf*. In fact it probably is a *waw*, which more easily explains its absence in *qf* in the second inscription on the ossuary and on the other ossuary. For when used as a vowel, the *waw* often drops out (as, for example, in *'lohim* 'God,' in biblical and post-biblical literature). However, a Caiaphas vocalization requires a consonantal *yod*, that is, *Qayapha*. The *yod* is not optional and therefore should not drop out. If *Qayapha* was intended, then it is hard to explain the absence of the *yod*. However, if the letter is a *waw* (and the *yod* and *waw* are notoriously difficult to distinguish in the Hebrew script of this period), then the two spellings *qwf* and *qf* are not difficult to explain. The incised names should be vocalized as either *Qopha* or *Qupha*.[15] That is to say, the inscription refers to one 'Joseph, son of Qopha' or 'Joseph, son of Qupha' (and even if we read *yod*, the vocalization could be *Qeypha*). There is in fact a person mentioned in Eusebius (*Hist. eccl.* 4.7.7), whose name in Greek transliteration is *Barkoph*, which in Aramaic would be *bar qoph* ('son of Qoph'). And the Qoph vocalization agrees with the oldest reading in the Mishnah (that is, *m. Parah* 3.5), in the oldest manuscripts.

A third reason for questioning the Caiaphas identification lies in the observation that Josephus does not actually call the high priest 'Joseph, *son* of Caiaphas'; he refers to him as 'Joseph Caiaphas' and 'Joseph *called* [Greek: *epikaloumenon*] Caiaphas'. So even if we accept the unlikely vocalization *Yehoseph bar Qayapha*, we really do not have a match with the high priest's name as given in Josephus. Although the high priestly identification is not conclusively ruled out, the difficulties are such that it is probably wise to leave the question open.

Only weeks after the above paragraphs were written the Israel Antiquities Authority announced (29 June 2011) the recovery of an ossuary that had been looted, on which are inscribed the words: 'Miriam, daughter of Yeshua, son of Qayapha, priest of Ma'aziah, from Beth 'Imri'. This intriguing new discovery may shed light on the two 'Caiaphas' ossuaries discovered 20 years ago. Scientific testing has confirmed the authenticity and antiquity of the inscribed words. Careful palaeographical study may be able to confirm the vocalization of the name of this priest. If it is vocalized *Qayapha* (instead of *Qopha* or *Qupha*), then we could have a match with Caiaphas. Indeed, we may have the ossuary of the granddaughter of the high priest who condemned Jesus. A forthcoming study of the new discovery will appear in the *Israel Exploration Journal*.

Israel's high priests appointed by Herodians and Roman governors

Ananel (37–36 BCE)

Aristobulus (35 BCE)

Jesus, son of Phiabi (?)

Simon, son of Boethus (?)

Matthias, son of Theophilus (?)

Joseph, son of Ellem (?)

Joazar, son of Boethus (4 BCE)

Eleazar, son of Boethus (4 BCE–?)

Jesus, son of See (?)

Annas, son of Sethi (6–15 CE)

Ishmael, son of Phiabi (15–16 CE)

Eleazar, son of Annas (16–17 CE)

Simon, son of Camithus (17–18 CE)

Joseph, called Caiaphas (18–37 CE)

Jonathan, son of Annas (37 CE)

Theophilus, son of Annas (37–41 CE)

Simon Cantheras, son of Boethus (41 CE–?)

Matthias, son of Annas (?)

Elionaeus, son of Cantheras (?)

Joseph, son of Camei (?–47 CE)

Ananias, son of Nebebaeus (47–59 CE)

Ishmael, son of Phiabi (59–61 CE)

Joseph Cabi, son of high priest Simon (61–62 CE)

Annas, son of Annas (62 CE)

Jesus, son of Damnaeus (62–63 CE)

Jesus, son of Gamaliel (63–64 CE)

Matthias, son of Theophilus (65–66 CE)

Phannias, son of Samuel (67 CE–?), appointed by the rebels

Before ending this discussion, mention should perhaps be made of inscriptional evidence that unambiguously relates to two high priests and perhaps to two more. The first concerns Theophilus, son of Annas (or Ananus) and brother-in-law of Caiaphas, whose name appears on the ossuary of Yehohanah, granddaughter of the high priest. The ossuary made its appearance in the antiquities market in 1983 and almost certainly was looted from a crypt either in Jerusalem or in nearby Hizma. The inscription is found on the decorated side of the ossuary, within the middle arch of three arches. It reads as follows:[16]

Yehohanah
Yehohanah, daughter of Yehohanan,
son of Theophilus the high priest

Theophilus was appointed to the office of high priest in 37 CE by Vitellius, who ordered Pontius Pilate to return to Rome in late 36 CE. According to Josephus, Vitellius 'deposed Jonathan [immediate successor to Caiaphas] from his office as high priest and conferred it on Jonathan's brother Theophilus' (*Ant.* 18.123).

The name Theophilus in the ossuary inscription is a transliteration of the Greek name Theophilos. Among Jews the name is relatively rare. The name appears in the *Letter of Aristeas* (49), but this character is fictional. The name appears in the Lukan evangelist's prefaces to the Gospel of Luke (1.3) and Acts (1.1), but this individual, who is a real person, not a symbol or metaphor, is probably not Jewish. The feminine form of the name appears in Greek (Theophila) and Hebrew (*tiplah*) on another ossuary.

On an ostracon found at Masada were inked the words:

A[nani]as the high priest, 'Aqavia his son   (Mas no. 461)

The inscription may refer to Ananias, son of Nedebaeus, who served as high priest from 47 to 59 CE. According to Josephus, 'Herod, king of Chalcis, now removed Joseph, the son of Camei, from the high priesthood and assigned the office to Ananias, the son of Nedebaeus, as successor' (*Ant.* 20.103). This may be the man mentioned in the New Testament, who orders Paul be struck (Acts 23.2–5). In the aftermath of the violence between Samaritans and Galileans and various accusations, Ananias was placed in chains and sent to Rome

(*Ant.* 20.131). The outcome of this trial is not clear. It is possible that the 'Eleazar, son of Ananias the high priest', who persuaded officials to discontinue sacrifices for Rome and the Roman Emperor (*J.W.* 2.409–10), was the son of Ananias, son of Nedebaeus.

The appearance of his name on an ostracon at Masada does not mean that the former high priest was numbered among the rebels during the war, or that he had been at Masada, or that he owned the jar on which his name has been found. It is speculated that his son 'Aqavia simply appealed to the prestige of his father, who had served as high priest, perhaps guaranteeing the purity of the contents of the jar.

We may have the name of a third high priest attested. On a circular stone weight found in the ruins of the 'Burnt House' (70 CE; Figure 4.6) in the old city of Jerusalem, not too far from the southwest corner of the Temple Mount, we find inscribed:

[of] the son of
Qatros

Figure 4.6 The 'Burnt House', Jerusalem
The so-called 'Burnt House' (Jewish Quarter of Old Jerusalem) may have belonged to a priestly family. The stone table and containers attest to the Jewish concern with purity. In one of the rooms, the skeletal remains of a woman's arm and the iron portion of a Roman spear were found. The house was destroyed in 70 CE.

The name may also be found inked on an ostracon from Masada. It reads: 'daughter of Qatra' (Mas no. 405).

The son of Qatros on the stone weight from Jerusalem and (somewhat less probably) the daughter of Qatra on the ostracon from Masada may have been members of one of the principal high priestly families that held sway in the last century or so of the Second Temple period. Later rabbis would remember these families in a critical light:

> Violent men of the priesthood came and took away [the tithes] by force . . . Concerning these and people like them . . . Abba Saul ben Bitnit and Abba Yose ben Yohanan of Jerusalem say: 'Woe is me because of the House of Boethos. Woe is me because of their clubs. Woe is me because of the house of Qadros. Woe is me because of their pen. Woe is me because of the house of Hanan [that is Annas]. Woe is me because of their whispering. Woe is me because of the house of Ishmael ben Phiabi.'   (*t. Menah.* 13.19, 21)

This activity of violence and theft is also described by Josephus:

> But Ananias [probably the son of Hanan, or Annas] had servants who were utter rascals and who, combining operations with the most reckless men, would go to the threshing floors and take by force the tithes of the priests; nor did they refrain from beating those who refused to give. The high priests were guilty of the same practices as his [Ananias'] slaves, and no one could stop them.   (*Ant.* 20.206)

This Qatros may be the Cantheras (Greek: Kantheras) mentioned by Josephus (*Ant.* 20.16). Attempts to identify Cantheras with Caiaphas are not persuasive.

And finally, we may also have the name of Boethos, whose name appeared above in the passage cited from the Tosefta. On an ossuary found on the western slope of Mount Scopus, Jerusalem, we find inscribed:

Boethos
    Shim'on, of [the family of] Boethos

Eleazar Sukenik links this inscription and ossuary to the family of Simon, son of Boethos of Alexandria,[17] whom Herod appointed to the high priesthood, in order to marry his daughter (Josephus, *Ant.* 15.320–22). The Qatros or Canteras mentioned above may have been his son. The Hebrew form *Boton*, Sukenik suggests, represents the genitive plural (Greek: *Boēthōn*) of Boethos. Accordingly, the inscription literally means 'Simon, of the Boethians'. Sukenik's suggestions are plausible and may well be correct, even if they remain unproven.

We may have inscriptional evidence of yet another member of this family. On an ossuary we have 'Yoezer, son of Simon' (*CIJ* no. 1354) and on ostraca from Masada we have 'Yoezer' (Mas no. 383) and 'Simeon ben Yoezer' (Mas no. 466). The affiliation of Yoezer and Simeon is significant in light of what Josephus relates: 'Jozar [= Yoezer], also a Pharisee, came of a priestly family; the youngest, Simon, was descended from high priests' (*Life* 197). This 'Jozar' may be the same person as Joazar, son of Boethos (Josephus, *Ant.* 17.164; 18.3), who himself served as high priest briefly in 4 BCE.

In the rabbinic passage cited above, it is said of the family of Boethos: 'Woe is me because of their clubs.' The tradition is probably recalling the violence some of the ruling priests practised against their lower-ranking brethren in the final years of the Second Temple. Josephus refers to this violence, though in reference to the high priest Ananias in the passage cited above (*Ant.* 20.206).

Some of Jesus' quarrels with the temple establishment centred on money. He is confronted in the temple precincts with a question about paying taxes: 'Should we, or shouldn't we?' (Mark 12.13–17). What many moderns may not know is that the provincial tribute tax was collected and housed in the treasury building on the Temple Mount (see Figure 4.7, overleaf). The peaceful collection of this tax was one of the primary responsibilities of the high priest and his high-ranking priestly associates.[18]

Jesus criticizes scribes in the temple precincts for 'devouring the houses of widows' (Mark 12.38–40) and utters a lament when the poor widow casts her last penny into the receptacle (Mark 12.41–44). Others criticized the ruling priests for their role in 'robbing the poor' (CD 6.15–17; 1QpHab 12.9–10; *T. Mos.* 5.3–6). None of this would have pleased the ruling priests. Moreover Jesus' condemnation of the practice of qorban, in which what is dedicated to the temple overrides care for one's parents, would have annoyed the temple establishment, which benefited from such vows. We in

Figure 4.7 Tyrian half sheqel
The Tyrian half sheqel was accepted at the temple for payment of the controversial 'half-sheqel tax'. See Matthew 17.24–27. Photograph courtesy of Anders Runesson.

fact have an inscription in which the word qorban appears with the same meaning as in Jesus' debate with the Pharisees. Let's look at this example.

In Mark 7.6–13 Jesus makes critical reference to the qorban tradition, whereby assets and property are consecrated or 'given' to God and are therefore no longer available for profane or secular use. In some cases, Pharisaic application of this tradition could have negative consequences. As Jesus puts it:

> you say, 'If a man tells his father or his mother, "What you would have gained from me is qorban"' (that is, given to God) – then you no longer permit him to do anything for his father or mother.
>
> (vv. 11–12)

In the past, commentators usually made reference to the mishnaic rules of qorban (esp. as spelled out in the tractate *Nedarim*).

However, four inscriptions have come to light that attest to the custom to which Jesus alluded and clarify it helpfully. In 1893 Father Marie-Joseph Lagrange published two of these inscriptions. The first is found on a limestone block (2.4 m by 40 cm) that had been discovered in the excavation of Mount Zion, near 'David's Gate'. The inscription is in Aramaic and it reads:

for the fire, a gift

Lagrange plausibly surmises that this inscription has to do with someone's vow to provide for the fire for the altar, as seen, for example, in *m. Ned.* 1.3 and other passages where qorban vows are discussed and the provision of fire for the altar is one of the examples.

Lagrange cites a second inscription, this one found on an ossuary discovered on the Mount of Olives. It reads:

for the fire, a gift
– Martha

The meaning here is probably the same as in the case of the first inscription. In this case the donor of the consecrated gift for the altar fire is a woman named Martha. Because her name and the inscription appear on an ossuary, it is possible that her gift was a bequest.[19]

In the aftermath of the 1967 Six Day War, which resulted in east Jerusalem falling into Israeli hands, a series of excavations got under way that uncovered the ruins of a mansion – the so-called 'Burnt House' – and a variety of other interesting finds. Securing the Western Wall of the Temple Mount finally made it possible to excavate safely in this area as well. In the vicinity of the southwest corner of the Herodian wall that supports the Temple Mount the fragment of a stone vessel – perhaps one of its legs – was uncovered that bore the inscribed word *qrbn*.[20]

The word *qorban* or 'gift' (*qrbn*) is found written along with pictures of two birds (the word, in fact, seems to be superimposed over the birds; Figure 4.8). Mazar wonders if use of this stone vessel had anything to do with Leviticus 12.8, the woman's offering after childbirth: 'And if she cannot afford a lamb, then she shall take two turtledoves or two young pigeons, one for a burnt offering and the other for a sin offering; and the priest shall make atonement for her, and she shall be clean.' Mazar also calls our attention to *m. Ma'aś. Š.* 4.10: 'One who finds a vessel upon which is inscribed [the word] "offering" [*qrbn*].'

Figure 4.8 Qorban inscription, Jerusalem
A stone with the word inscribed *qrbn* (qorban), 'gift', found in Jerusalem.
Photograph courtesy of Anders Runesson.

It is the fourth inscription, found on an ossuary that was discovered in 1956, first published and discussed by Józef Tadeusz
Milik, that has given us what is probably the parallel to Jesus'
reference to qorban in Mark 7. The inscription, found on the lid of
the ossuary, is in Aramaic and probably dates to the first century
BCE. Joseph Fitzmyer has transcribed and translated the inscription
as follows:

> Everything that a man will find to his profit in this ossuary [is]
> an offering to God from the one within it.[21]

Qrbn is translated 'an offering', its normal meaning. Milik thought
the inscription pronounced a curse on anyone who pilfered the
contents of the ossuary, so he translated: 'Whoever will re-use this
ossuary to his profit, may there be a curse of God on behalf of him
who is inside!' Milik acknowledges that *qrbn* is literally 'offering'. But
he understands this offering in an imprecatory sense, as we sometimes
see in rabbinic use of the synonym *qonam* (for example *m. Ned.* 4.5).
Fitzmyer rightly finds this reasoning unconvincing.

He thinks it better to understand the inscription as a close parallel
to Mark 7.11. 'The new inscription does not alter the sense of the

word in Matthew or Mark but provides a perfect contemporary parallel.' He is correct. The qorban inscription thus provides a valuable parallel to part of Jesus' teaching, which in this instance stands in tension with Pharisaic halakah and may have had – from the point of view of the ruling priests – worrisome implications for the temple establishment.

Finally, there are two other closely related aspects of Jesus' ministry that may not have been appreciated by the priesthood: healing and forgiveness of sins. The latter is not hard to understand. Jesus says to the paralysed man who has been lowered through the roof of the house in which he was teaching (Mark 2.1–12): 'My son, your sins are forgiven' (v. 6). The scribes who are present are shocked and ask: 'Why does this man speak thus? It is blasphemy! Who can forgive sins but God alone?' (v. 7). Not only is God the one who forgives sins (Exod. 34.6–7; Isa. 43.25), his forgiveness is announced through the priests and the sacrificial system (Exod. 30.10; Lev. 4.3), and on one occasion a prophet (2 Sam. 12.13). In effect Jesus has usurped the priestly function. The scribes had challenged Jesus' authority and he met the challenge by healing the paralysed man, something far more difficult than merely mouthing the words, 'Your sins are forgiven.' Priests can do this, but can they say to the sick, 'Rise, take up your pallet and walk' (vv. 9, 11)?

We see this again when Jesus heals the leper (Mark 1.40–45). The leper kneels before Jesus, beseeching him: 'If you will, you can make me clean' (v. 40). Jesus replies, 'I will; be clean' (v. 41). Jesus may have implicitly challenged priestly authority but he nevertheless respects the law of Moses. He commands the healed man: 'Go, show yourself to the priest, and offer for your cleansing what Moses commanded, for a testimony to the people' (v. 44). Jesus pronounces the man clean but orders him to comply with Moses (Lev. 13.6, 13, 23, etc.). After all, according to Moses a person is not 'clean' (or free from leprosy) until the priest inspects him and says he is clean. To this point Jesus has respected both Moses and the role of the village priest. But he also says that the man is to do this as a 'testimony' (*marturian*) to the people. A testimony? In what sense? Implicit in this instruction is a challenge. The healed man is to comply with the law of Moses, but in complying (and being declared clean by the village priest), the people know that it was by the authority of Jesus that the man was cleansed of his leprosy. The priest can only confirm what Jesus has done and what Jesus himself pronounced: 'Be clean'.

Some interpreters have suggested that there was no leprosy in the time of Jesus, that Hansen's Disease became known in the Middle East at a later date. However, thanks to archaeology there is now dramatic evidence of its existence in the early first century. Scientific testing of the burial shroud in the so-called 'Shroud Tomb' has confirmed the presence of leprosy. The shroud was discovered in 2000 in Akeldama in the lower Hinnom Valley in Jerusalem. The tomb was discovered quite by chance, thanks in part to the presence of freshly broken ossuaries – evidence of recent vandalism. Shimon Gibson entered the tomb and found that many of its ossuaries and skeletal contents had been smashed. Fortunately the remains of a skeleton, wrapped in a shroud, were lying undisturbed in a niche. Not only were portions of the shroud still intact but clumps of human hair were attached to it. It was a remarkable find.

Accelerator Mass Spectrometry (AMS) radio carbon dating confirmed the first-century date of both shroud and skeletal remains. DNA testing confirmed that the man wrapped in the shroud was related to other members whose skeletal remains were recovered in the tomb. This DNA testing also revealed that the man had suffered from leprosy (*Mycobacterium Leprae* or Hansen's Disease), though his immediate cause of death was from the complications of tuberculosis (it is not uncommon for sufferers of leprosy also to contract tuberculosis). Because of the high quality of the tomb and its location near other tombs of high quality, Gibson deduces – rightly in my opinion – that the man who suffered from leprosy was from an aristocratic family and perhaps was a member of the priestly aristocracy.[22] In this amazing discovery we have further evidence that wealth and power did not confer immunity from serious disease and illness. In any case, the man found in the Shroud Tomb confirms the presence of leprosy in Israel in the time of Jesus.

Medical examination of the remains of hundreds of people from the time of Jesus has revealed evidence of high infant mortality and widespread illness, such as caused from parasites. The skeletal evidence indicates that 48 per cent of those interred in the Akeldama tomb did not reach adulthood and that several who did suffered from various infirmities, including those caused by parasites such as tapeworm, as indicated by the calcified cysts left behind. Anthropologist Joe Zias, who has examined the remains of hundreds of people from late antiquity, remarks that 'the relative wealth of the families buried here, manifested by tomb architecture and the ossuaries, did not confer any significant health advantages'.

It might be mentioned that the forensic evidence from the so-called Caiaphas tomb is similar. This tomb contained the remains of approximately 63 persons (looting makes an exact body count impossible). Only one-third of these persons reached adulthood, and some skeletons exhibited signs of degenerative disease.[23] Indeed, the Tomb of Jason – a large, ornate complex – offers many features of interest.[24] Again, forensic evidence is suggestive. Of the 25 individuals interred in this tomb only three lived beyond the age of 25 (ten died by the age of 12). Life expectancy was short in the time of Jesus – more than half died before reaching 30.[25]

The evidence from these tombs, though admittedly as a sample quite limited in time and place, nevertheless does assist us in better appreciating the healing dimension in Jesus' ministry. If the wealthy, who have access to the best physicians and medicines, were no better off than the inmates of the Akeldama, Caiaphas and Jason tombs, it's not hard to see why Jesus, who enjoyed the reputation of a healer, drew large crowds that at times actually interfered with his activities (for example Mark 1.28, 32–34, 36–37, 45; 2.1–4; 3.7–12; 4.1). Even the wealthy would likely have sought aid from Jesus, as perhaps in the case of the synagogue official (Mark 5.21–24) or the woman of means who had spent much on doctors (Mark 5.25–26).

There is another dimension to Jesus' success as healer and exorcist and the widespread fame that went with this success. Because he could heal more effectively than the scribes and priests (and never demanded payment!), and because he dared to pronounce people forgiven, whole, clean and 'released', it is not too surprising that he made some enemies along the way. But it is one thing to trespass against scribes or village priests, quite another to offend the aristocratic priesthood of Jerusalem. This will be one of the topics in Chapter 5.

5

Life with the dead:
Jewish burial traditions

The Jewish people buried their dead, then later gathered the bones and placed them in containers called ossuaries or a vault set aside for this purpose. The practice of gathering the bones of the deceased is called ossilegium or secondary burial (*y. Mo'ed Qat.* 1.5, 80c: 'At first they would bury them in ditches, and when the flesh had decayed, they would gather the bones and bury them in ossuaries'). How far back this practice may be traced and where it originated are major questions that lie at the heart of the debate surrounding the significance of the numerous ossuaries found in and around Jerusalem, dating to the Herodian period (*c*.35 BCE–70 CE).[1]

In my view, the most plausible explanation for the dramatic increase in the number of ossuaries put into use in the time of Herod the Great and his successors is that it had to do with Herod's extensive building projects in and around Jerusalem, especially those concerned with the Temple Mount and the new Sanctuary (see Josephus, *Ant.* 15.390). The Temple Mount was enormous and included a series of buildings and colonnades, with the Sanctuary itself the most impressive of all of the structures. Josephus emphasizes the size and beauty of the stones (for example *Ant.* 15.399; Mark 13.1: 'Look, Teacher, what large stones and what large buildings!'). Although the Sanctuary itself and other key structures were completed in Herod's lifetime, work on the Temple Mount continued until 64 CE, throughout the respective administrations of his surviving sons, his grandson Agrippa I and his great-grandson Agrippa II. Accordingly the meaning of the remark in John 2.20 implies ongoing construction and not completion. It should read: 'This temple has been under construction for forty-six years.' When work on the Temple Mount was finally completed, Josephus tells us that 18,000 workers were laid off (*Ant.* 20.219). This massive layoff contributed to the growing social and political instability that just two years later exploded into open rebellion.

It is in this chronological coincidence between Herod's massive building programme, which employed thousands of stonecutters during his reign (in the 30s BCE to 64 CE), and the appearance of thousands of ossuaries, carved from the same type of stone (limestone) from which almost all of the Temple Mount buildings were fashioned, that we find the answer to our question. The number of ossuaries that were made of limestone increased dramatically during the one century of temple-related building in Jerusalem, not because of a shift in theology or foreign influence but because of the great number of stonecutters, quarries and rejected blocks of limestone. The increase of the city's population and its urban and suburban sprawl also encouraged greater density in burial sites. Simply put, more dead relatives can be interred in the family vault if they are placed in ossuaries than if they are left lying in niches or in full-sized sarcophagi. Although these factors came into play primarily in Jerusalem, their influence may account for the appearance of ossuaries in Jericho and elsewhere during this period.

How the Jewish people buried their dead

So what were Jewish burial practices in the first century? First, burial took place on the day of death or, if death occurred at the end of the day or during the night, the following day. Knowing this lends a great deal of pathos to some otherwise familiar Gospel stories. We think of the story of the widow from the city of Nain: 'As he approached the gate of the town, a man who had died was being carried out. He was his mother's only son and she was a widow; and with her was a large crowd from the town' (Luke 7.12). Her only son had died that day (or the evening before). Her sorrow is at its rawest when Jesus encounters her. We also think of the desperate father who hurries Jesus to his home, hoping he will arrive in time to heal his dying daughter: 'Jesus came to the leader's house and saw the flute players and the crowd making a commotion' (Matt. 9.23). As it turns out, by the time they arrive the girl has died and the funeral process, complete with music and weeping, is already under way.

Following death, the body was washed and wrapped. We can find this custom mentioned in several episodes in the Gospels and elsewhere. We see it in the story of Lazarus, who was bound and wrapped with cloths (John 11.44). The body of Jesus is wrapped in a clean linen shroud (Matt. 27.59; Luke 23.53; John 19.40). The body of Ananias is wrapped and buried (Acts 5.6); so also Dorcas, who 'became ill and died. When they had washed her, they laid her in a room upstairs' (Acts 9.37). Moreover the corpse was usually perfumed (Josephus, *Ant.* 15.61; for spices, see *Ant.* 17.196–99; John 19.39–40).

The day of burial was the first of seven days of mourning (*Semahot* 12.1). This is clearly stated by first-century Jewish historian Josephus in reference to the death, burial and funeral of Herod the Great (d. 4 BCE): 'Now Archelaus [Herod's oldest surviving son] continued to mourn for seven days out of respect for his father – the custom of the country prescribes this number of days – and then, after feasting the crowds and making an end of the mourning, he went up to the temple' (*Ant.* 17.200). The custom of seven days of mourning arose from Scripture itself: Joseph 'observed a time of mourning for his father seven days' (Gen. 50.10); and in reference to the remains of king Saul and his sons, Israelite men 'took their bones and buried them under the tamarisk tree in Jabesh, and fasted seven days' (1 Sam. 31.13).

Mourning normally took place at the tomb's entrance or within the tomb itself. This is why archaeologists sometimes find a portion of the floor carved out more deeply, allowing mourners to pray standing upright, according to the Jewish custom (see the tomb open for viewing at Dominus Flevit on the Mount of Olives, Figure 5.1). Of course, standing inside the tomb was why the corpse was perfumed. Many perfume bottles and jars have been found in tombs and burial caves. One can only imagine how unpleasant the tomb would have become by the sixth and seventh days.

One year after death it was customary to gather the bones and place them in a bone niche or in an ossuary. As noted, this is sometimes called secondary burial, and is readily observed in the archaeological excavations of Jewish tombs in the time of Jesus. It is also attested in later rabbinic literature: 'When the flesh had wasted away they gathered together the bones and buried them in their own place'

Figure 5.1 Ossuaries, Mount of Olives
The interior of a burial crypt at Dominus Flevit ('The Lord wept') on
the Mount of Olives. Most of the ossuaries, in which the bones of the
dead were gathered and reburied, are of adult size. Child-sized ossuaries
are rare because the skeletal remains of children were usually placed
with those of adult relatives in larger ossuaries. Photograph courtesy of
Anders Runesson.

(*m. Sanh.* 6.6); 'My son, bury me at first in a niche. In the course of
time, collect my bones and put them in an ossuary but do not
gather them with your own hands' (*Semahot* 12.9; see also *Semahot*
3.2). The custom of the interval of 12 months from primary to
secondary burial is also attested in rabbinic literature (*b. Qidd.*
31b).

For executed criminals, however, the rules were different. Criminals
were to be buried properly, but not in places of honour such as the
family tomb. This is clearly taught in the earliest writings of the Rabbis:
'They did not bury [the executed criminal] in the burying-place of

his fathers. But two burying-places were kept in readiness by the Sanhedrin, one for them that were beheaded or strangled, and one for them that were stoned or burnt' (*m. Sanh.* 6.5); 'Neither a corpse nor the bones of a corpse may be transferred from a wretched place to an honoured place, nor, needless to say, from an honoured placed to a wretched place; but if to the family tomb, even from an honoured place to a wretched place, it is permitted' (*Semahot* 13.7). Not only was the body of a criminal not to be buried in a place of honour, no public mourning for executed criminals was permitted: 'they used not to make [open] lamentation . . . for mourning has place in the heart alone' (*m. Sanh.* 6.6).

The Jewish people believed that the soul of the deceased lingered near the corpse for three days: 'For three days [after death] the soul hovers over the body, intending to re-enter it, but as soon as it sees its appearance change, it departs' (*Lev. Rab.* 18.1 (on Lev. 15.1–2)). The change of the face on the third day explains, we are told, why the grief is felt most in the early days of mourning: 'The full intensity of mourning lasts up to the third day because the appearance of the face is still recognizable' (*Qoh. Rab.* 12.6 §1). This interesting belief likely lies behind the dramatic story of the raising of Lazarus, brother of Mary and Martha (John 11.1–44). The comments that Lazarus has been dead 'four days' and that by now his corpse 'stinks' (11.39) imply that all hope is now lost. Lazarus has been dead for more than three days. His spirit has departed; his face has changed its appearance. Resuscitation, it was assumed, is no longer possible.

These are the burial customs of the Jewish people. But did the Jewish people always bury the dead? Was burial important to them? Were they willing to leave people unburied, such as executed criminals?

The necessity of burial

In the Mediterranean world of late antiquity, proper burial of the dead was regarded as sacred duty, especially in the culture and religion of the Jewish people. The first reason for providing proper burial was for the sake of the dead themselves. The importance of care for the dead and their proper burial is well attested in Scripture, from the amount of attention given to the story of Abraham's purchase of a cave for the burial of Sarah (Gen. 23.4–19) to the burial accounts of the patriarchs and monarchs of Israel. Of special interest is the story of Jacob's body taken to the land of Canaan to be buried in a tomb that he had hewn (Gen. 50.4–14). So also Joseph: though buried in Egypt, his bones were exhumed and taken with the Israelites at the time of the exodus to be buried eventually in Canaan (Gen. 50.22–26; Josh. 24.32). The bones of the slain Saul and sons were buried in Jabesh (1 Sam. 31.12–13). The king's bones were later taken to the land of Benjamin (2 Sam. 21.12–14). Even the wicked and divinely judged were buried too, such as those in the wilderness who were greedy for meat (Num. 11.33–34) or individual criminals who were executed (Deut. 21.22–23). Israel's enemies, slain in battle, were buried (1 Kings 11.15). Even the eschatological enemy hosts of Gog are to be buried (Ezek. 39.11–16). To leave the dead, even enemy dead, lying about unburied was to bring a curse on the land (Deut. 21.22–23).

The ghastly image of Jews in exile, murdered and then left unburied beside the road or flung outside the city walls, is reflected in the book of Tobit. The book's namesake is a righteous man who observes Jewish food laws, shares food and clothing with the poor and buries the dead, even at great personal risk. Indeed, Tobit's burying the dead was his greatest virtue (1.18–20; 2.3–8; 4.3–4; 6.15; 14.10–13).

Josephus' perspective is consistent with that expressed in Tobit. Explaining Jewish ethical obligations, Josephus states: 'We must furnish fire, water, food to all who ask for them, point out the road, not leave a corpse unburied [*ataphon*], show consideration even to declared enemies' (*Ag. Ap.* 2.211; see also 2.205).

Perhaps Philo gives the most eloquent expression to Jewish sensitivities on this question, in his imaginative recounting of Jacob's grief over the report that his son Joseph had been killed and devoured by wild animals. The patriarch laments:

> Child, it is not your death that grieves me, but the manner of it. If you had been buried [*etaphēs*] in your own land, I should have been comforted and watched and nursed your sick-bed, exchanged the last farewells as you died, closed your eyes, wept over your body as it lay there, given it a costly funeral and left none of the customary rites undone.
> (*Joseph* 22–23)

The imaginative dirge goes on to speak of the importance of proper burial:

> And, indeed, if you had to die by violence or through premeditation, it would have been a lighter ill to me, slain as you would have been by human beings, who would have pitied their dead victim, gathered some dust and covered the corpse. And then if they had been the cruellest of men, what more could they have done but cast it out unburied and go their way, and then perhaps some passer-by would have stayed his steps, and, as he looked, felt pity for our common nature and deemed the custom of burial to be its due. (*Joseph* 25)

Jacob concludes his lament by saying that he has experienced no greater tragedy, in that nothing of Joseph remains and that there is no possibility of burial (26–27). Jewish sensitivities with respect to proper burial could hardly have been given more eloquent expression than what we find here in Philo.

Concern with proper burial continues beyond the first century. For the Rabbis, burial of the dead was regarded as a sacred duty (*b. Meg.* 3b), taking precedence over the study of the law, the circumcision of one's son or the offering of the Passover lamb. Indeed, even a high priest or a Nazirite has the obligation to bury a 'neglected corpse' since there is no one else to do it (*Sipre Num.* §26 (on Num. 6.6–8)).

A second reason for burying the dead is to avoid defilement of the land of Israel. This requirement is grounded in the Mosaic law:

> When someone is convicted of a crime punishable by death and is executed, and you hang him on a tree, his corpse must not remain all night upon the tree; you shall bury him that same day, for anyone hung on a tree is under God's curse. You must not defile the land that the Lord your God is giving you for possession.
>
> (Deut. 21.22–23)

It is also expressed in Ezekiel: 'They will set apart men to pass through the land regularly and bury any invaders who remain on the face of the land, so as to cleanse it . . . Thus they shall cleanse the land' (Ezek. 39.14, 16).

This tradition remained current at the turn of the era, as seen in its elaboration in the Temple Scroll, one of the Dead Sea Scrolls, where we read:

If a man is a traitor against his people and gives them up to a foreign nation, so doing evil to his people, *you are to hang him on a tree until dead*. On the testimony of two or three witnesses he will be put to death, and they themselves shall hang him on the tree. If a man is convicted of a capital crime and flees to the nations, cursing his people and the children of Israel, *you are to hang him, also, upon a tree until dead*. But you must not let their bodies remain on the tree overnight; you shall most certainly bury them that very day. Indeed, anyone hung on a tree is accursed of God and men, but you are not to defile the land that I am about to give you as an inheritance [Deut. 21.22–23].

(11QTemple 64.7–13a = 4Q524 frag. 14, lines 2–4; emphasis added)

Whereas Deuteronomy 21.22–23 speaks of one put to death and then hanged, 11QTemple speaks of one hanged 'until dead'. Most think crucifixion is in view in this latter instance (as also in 4QpNah frags 3–4, col. i, lines 6–8, and perhaps also in 4Q282i, which refers to the hanging up (probably crucifixion) of those who lead the people astray).[2] It is also important to note that this form of execution is linked to treason.

Roman emperors during the Herodian period

Julius Caesar (48–44 BCE)

Caesar Augustus (31 BCE–14 CE)

Tiberius (14–37 CE)

Gaius Caligula (37–41 CE)

Claudius (41–54 CE)

Nero (54–68 CE)

Galba, Otho, Vitellius (68–69 CE)

Vespasian (69–79 CE)

Titus (79–81 CE)

Domitian (81–96 CE)

Nerva (96–98 CE)

Trajan (98–117 CE)

Hadrian (117–138 CE)

It should also be observed that the requirement to bury the executed person *the day of his death* is emphasized. In Deuteronomy it simply says, 'you shall bury him the same day'; but the Temple Scroll adds, 'you must not let their bodies remain on the tree overnight'. The reason given for taking the bodies down and burying them the day (or evening) of death is to avoid defiling the land, for the executed person is 'cursed of God'. This is probably the rationale that lies behind the concern regarding slain enemy soldiers.

In a section concerned with holiness, the Temple Scroll enjoins Israel:

> 'for you are a people holy to the Lord your God' [Deut. 14.2]. 'Thus you shall not defile your land' [Num. 35.34]. You are not to do as the nations do: they bury their dead everywhere, even inside their homes. Rather, you must set apart places in your land where you will bury your dead. For every four cities you must designate one burial ground.
> (11QTemple 48.10–14)

What is important here is that even in the case of the executed criminal, proper burial was anticipated. Various restrictions may have applied, such as being forbidden burial in one's family tomb – at least until the flesh had decomposed – or not being allowed to mourn publicly, but burial was to take place, in keeping with the scriptural command of Deuteronomy 21.22–23 and the Jewish customs that had grown up alongside it.

The commands of Scripture, taken with traditions regarding piety (as especially exemplified in Tobit), corpse impurity and the avoidance of the defilement of the land, strongly suggest that under normal circumstances – that is, peacetime – no corpse would remain unburied, neither Jew nor Gentile, innocent nor guilty. *All* were to be buried. What is especially interesting is that some of the tradition reviewed above may have been specifically linked to, even produced by, priests – as in the materials from Qumran. If this is the case then the relevance of these laws and traditions for the execution of Jesus of Nazareth and its aftermath becomes more evident, for it was the ruling priesthood that condemned Jesus to death and would have primary responsibility for seeing to the proper burial of his body.

We have reviewed the most important literary evidence concerning Jewish attitudes towards burial. What can we learn from the archaeological evidence?

The archaeological evidence of burial in the Roman era

As it so happens, there is significant archaeological evidence that has a direct bearing on the question of whether the body of Jesus of Nazareth, crucified by order of Pontius Pilate, was placed in a tomb, as the Gospels say it was. As we shall see, the evidence suggests that Jesus was indeed buried, in keeping with Jewish customs, Roman tolerance of Jewish customs and the views expressed by all Christian and non-Christian literature from late antiquity. There is in fact not one shred of evidence from antiquity that suggests Jesus was not buried, which makes it all the more curious how these ideas and rumours to the contrary persist.

The important discovery in 1968 of an ossuary (ossuary no. 4 in Tomb I, at Giv'at ha-Mivtar) of a Jewish man named Yehohanan,

Figure 5.2 Pilate Stone, Caesarea Maritima
The stone, unearthed in 1961 at Caesarea Maritima, has incised on it the words '[Pon]tius Pilate, [pref]ect of Judea'. This discovery settled the question of Pilate's rank; he was a prefect, not a procurator.

who had obviously been crucified, provides archaeological evidence and insight into how Jesus himself may have been crucified. The ossuary and its contents date to the late 20s CE; that is, during the administration of Pilate, the very Roman prefect who condemned Jesus to the cross (Figure 5.2, p. 122). The remains of an iron spike 11.5 cm long are plainly seen still encrusted in the right heel bone or calcaneum (Figure 5.3, overleaf). Those who took down the body of Yehohanan were apparently unable to remove the spike, with the result that a piece of wood, from an olive tree, remained affixed to it. Later the skeletal remains of the body – spike, fragment of wood and all – were placed in the ossuary. Forensic examination of the rest of the skeletal remains supports the view that Yehohanan was crucified with arms apart, hung from a horizontal beam or tree branch. However, there is no evidence that his arms or wrists were nailed to this crossbeam.

The Roman governors

Prefects of Samaria and Judea

Coponius (6–9 CE)
Marcus Ambibulus (9–12 CE)
Annius Rufus (12–15 CE)
Valerius Gratus (15–19/25 CE)
Pontius Pilate (19/25–37 CE)
Marcellus (37 CE)
Marullus (37–41 CE)

Procurators of all Israel

Fadus (44–46 CE)
Tiberius Alexander (46–48 CE)
Ventidius Cumanus (48–52 CE)
Felix (52–60 CE)
Porcius Festus (60–62 CE)
Albinus (62–64 CE)
Gessius Florus (64–66 CE)

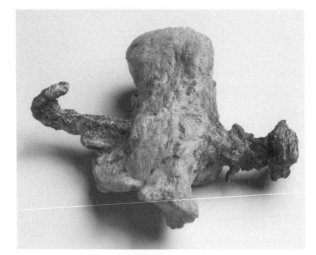

Figure 5.3 Heel bone of a crucified man
The right heel, transfixed by an iron spike, of one Yehohanan, crucified
in the first century, probably during the administration of Pontius
Pilate, governor of Samaria and Judea. Despite Yehohanan's execution
as a criminal, the authorities permitted his family to gather and rebury
his skeletal remains in the family tomb. Photograph courtesy of the
Israel Museum, Jerusalem.

The lack of nails or spikes in the hands or wrists of Yehohanan
is consistent with a reference in Pliny the Elder (23–79 CE), who
refers to rope being used in crucifixion (*Nat.* 28.4). Nevertheless, it
is recorded by others that many victims of crucifixion did have their
hands or wrists nailed to the beam. Writing in the second century
BCE, Plautus refers to the crucifixion victim, 'his arms and legs are
double-nailed' (*Mostellaria* 359–61). A third-century CE author
described it this way: 'Punished with limbs outstretched . . . they are
fastened (and) nailed to the stake in the most bitter torment, evil
food for birds of prey and grim picking for dogs' (*Apotelesmatica*
4.198–200). Recall the Latin graffiti examined in Chapter 3; one,
inscribed on the wall of a bath house in Pompeii, reads: 'May you
be nailed to the cross!' (*CIL* IV.2082). Another in Pompeii reads:
'Cornelius, get hung!' (*CIL* IV.1864).

Yehohanan's leg bones were broken, but there is disagreement over
how and when; that is, while still on the cross or after being taken

down. Some think that the breaks in the lower leg bones, including the cut to the talus bone of the foot, are due to *crurifragium*, the breaking of a victim's bones to hasten his death. Others do not think the talus suffered such an injury. Indeed, the talus under question may actually belong to one of the other two individuals whose skeletal remains had been placed in the ossuary. Accordingly, the conclusion that Yehohanan's leg bones were broken before death and decarnation is disputed. Because of the age and degraded condition of the skeletal materials, some uncertainty remains.[3]

If Yehohanan's legs were broken before death, we then know not only that he was taken down and buried (as indicated by the discovery of his remains in an ossuary), but also that his death was intentionally hastened. The most likely and compelling reason for hastening death in this manner was so that his corpse could be taken down from the cross and placed in a tomb before nightfall, as Scripture commands (Deut. 21.22–23) and as Jewish custom required. The Romans had no reason of their own to expedite death by crucifixion; they would prefer just the opposite – a long, drawn-out death.

Also found in the tombs discovered at Giv'at Ha-Mivtar were the remains of a woman(?) who had been decapitated. Whether she was murdered or executed is not clear.[4] (Below I shall give reasons why I think she was probably executed.) However, we may have the skeletal remains of another person who, like Yehohanan, was executed and whose remains eventually were placed in a family tomb. These remains were found in a cluster of tombs on Mount Scopus, north of Jerusalem. In Tomb C the skeletal remains of a woman (aged 50–60) give clear evidence of having been attacked – her right elbow suffered a deep cut that severed the end of the humerus. Because there is no sign of regrowth or infection, it is surmised that she died from the attack.

In Tomb D, which contains the remains of persons related to those interred in Tomb C, were the remains of a man (aged 50) who had been decapitated. It is plausible to speculate that this man had been executed, quite possibly for having murdered the female relative in Tomb C. However, physical anthropologist Joe Zias doubts that the man had been executed because his neck had been struck twice. Being struck twice, he reasons, suggests an act of violence rather than a judicial execution.[5] Zias could be correct, of course, but we should not assume that judicial beheadings were always neatly done.

One only needs to be reminded of the several badly aimed strokes that finally took off the head of James, Duke of Monmouth, in 1685. Apparently the executioner was intoxicated – his first stroke buried the axe in the Duke's shoulder! Mary Queen of Scots fared no better a century earlier, when in 1586 her cousin, Elizabeth I, had her executed for treason – it took the executioner three strokes to take off her head.

Forgive me for dwelling on such gruesome details, but I think there is an important point to be made here. Multiple cuts, as others might contend, do not in fact argue against interpreting beheadings as judicial executions. I have reviewed the evidence of hundreds of Roman-era skeletons that have been excavated – mostly in Britain, though some in Africa – and that have been found to have suffered decapitation. In about half the cases two or more strokes of the sword or axe were required before the head was separated from the body.

Of special interest for this topic was the discovery of the mass grave left behind by the bloody battle of Towton in fifteenth-century Britain. Although dating from a much later period, the skeletal remains are nevertheless quite instructive because the weapons employed and the manner of fighting were essentially the same as those from the earlier Roman period. Approximately half the several hundred slain had suffered fatal head wounds, and the other half had suffered fatal sword or spear thrusts through the body. Only one victim suffered decapitation, and it may have been a post-mortem insult, not the actual cause of death.[6] The point is this: if no one – or at most only one – was decapitated in pitched battle, where combatants were armed with axes and swords, what is the probability that someone suffered decapitation in a domestic alter-cation? I think it is rather slim.

Accordingly, the man in Giv‘at Ha-Mivtar Tomb D is probably another individual who suffered the death penalty – even if it took two strokes to finish the job – and whose skeletal remains were in due course placed in the family tomb. With all due respect to Joe Zias, I believe this means that we have apparently found three executed persons – one by crucifixion and two by beheading – who were buried according to Jewish customs in the time of Jesus. This means that they were given primary burial – most likely in a place of dishonour; that is, in one of the tombs reserved for executed criminals – and subsequently their skeletal remains were gathered and placed in ossuaries, which in turn were placed in their family burial vaults, all according to the laws and customs related in ancient Jewish literature.

But why have we found the buried remains of only three or four executed Jews in pre-70 CE Israel? Surely many more than these were executed. And if other executed persons were buried properly, as I have argued they would have been, then why have we not found many more skeletons of executed persons? Accordingly it has been argued by some that, in the light of the thousands of Jews crucified in the first century in the vicinity of Jerusalem, the discovery of only one properly buried crucifixion victim is proof that the normal Roman practice of not permitting burial must have obtained, even in Jewish Palestine. On the basis of this logic perhaps one should conclude that Jesus was not buried either.[7]

There are at least four objections that must be raised against this inference. First, almost all of the bones recovered from the time of Jesus are poorly preserved, especially the smaller bones of the feet and hands, which will normally provide evidence, if any, of crucifixion. It was the presence of the nail in the right heel of Yehohanan that made it clear that he had been crucified. The presence of the nail was a fluke. It was due to the sharp end being bent back (like a fishhook), perhaps because the nail struck a knot in the upright beam. When Yehohanan was taken down from the cross, the nail could not be extracted. So no statistics should be inferred from this unusual find.

Second, many crucifixion victims were scourged, beaten and then tied to the cross, not nailed. Thus skeletal remains would leave no trace of the trauma of crucifixion. Accordingly we do not know that Yehohanan is the only crucifixion victim discovered in a tomb – several others may have been found without our knowing it.

Third, the best-preserved skeletons are found in the better-constructed tombs, within bone pits or in ossuaries. These tombs were mostly those of the rich, not the poor. The poor were usually buried in the ground or in smaller natural caves. Not many of their skeletons have been found. The significance of this point is that it is the poor who are most likely to be crucified, not the wealthy and powerful. So those skeletons most likely to provide evidence of crucifixion are the skeletons least likely to survive, whereas the best-preserved skeletons are the ones least likely to have belonged to those who had been crucified.

Fourth, the vast majority of the thousands of Jews crucified and left unburied in the first century, in the vicinity of Jerusalem, died during the rebellion of 66–70 CE. They were not buried because Rome was at war with the Jewish people and had no wish to accommodate Jewish sensitivities, as it normally did during peacetime. It was during peacetime – indeed, during the administration of Pontius Pilate – that both Yehohanan and Jesus of Nazareth were crucified. That both were buried according to Jewish customs should hardly occasion surprise. Jewish priestly authorities were expected to defend the purity of Jerusalem (or at least give the appearance of doing so), while Roman authorities acquiesced to Jewish customs and sensitivities, as Philo and Josephus relate.

The archaeological evidence suggests that Jesus and other Jews executed in peacetime Israel were buried – not in honour but properly – in accordance with Jewish laws and customs. In the case of Jesus of Nazareth the expectation would have been to collect his skeletal remains approximately one year after death and transfer them from the place of dishonour to a place of honour, such as his family tomb or burial place. Historical and literary records can tell us more.

Burial and non-burial of executed criminals in the Roman world

The objection raised against the Gospels' story of the burial of Jesus rests primarily in the observation that victims of Roman crucifixion were normally not buried, but their corpses were left hanging on the cross, to be picked apart by birds and animals. That this is the normal Roman practice is not in dispute here. Martin Hengel has assembled most of the pertinent material. A few examples may be cited: 'The vulture hurries from dead cattle and dogs and crosses to bring some of the carrion to her offspring' (Juvenal, *Satires* 14.77–78); 'the carrion-birds will soon take care of' one's 'burial' (Suetonius, *Augustus* 13.1–2); 'hanging on a cross to feed crows' (Horace, *Epistles* 1.16.48); and the already cited text that describes the crucifixion victim as 'evil food for birds of prey and grim picking for dogs' (*Apotelesmatica* 4.200). On a second-century epitaph the deceased declares that his murderer, a slave, was 'crucified alive for the wild beasts and birds' (Amyzon Epitaph, Cave 1). Many other texts spare readers such gruesome details, but do mention the denial of proper burial (for example Livy 29.9.10; 29.18.14).

What is questioned here, though, is the assumption on the part of a few scholars that the hundreds, even thousands, of Jews crucified and left hanging on crosses outside the walls of Jerusalem, during the siege of 69–70 CE, are indicative of normal practice in Roman Palestine.[8] A review of Josephus suggests, to the contrary, that leaving the bodies of the executed unburied was *exceptional* not *typical*. It was, in fact, a departure from normal Roman practice in Jewish Palestine.

Peacetime administration in Palestine appears to have respected Jewish burial sensitivities. Indeed both Philo and Josephus claim that Roman administration acquiesced to Jewish customs. In his appeal to Caesar, Philo draws attention to the Jews who 'appealed to Pilate to redress the infringement of their traditions caused by the shields and not to disturb the customs which throughout all the preceding ages had been safeguarded without disturbance by kings and by emperors' (*Embassy* 300). A generation later Josephus asserts the same thing. The Romans, he says, do not require 'their subjects to violate their national laws' (*Ag. Ap.* 2.73). Josephus adds that the Roman procurators who succeeded Agrippa I 'by abstaining from all interference with the customs of the country kept the nation at peace' (*J.W.* 2.220).

The actions of Herod Antipas, with respect to John the Baptist, are consistent with this policy. Although the Baptist is executed by the tetrarch, his disciples are nonetheless allowed to bury his body (Mark 6.14–29; Josephus, *Ant.* 18.119).

Even Roman justice outside the Jewish setting sometimes permitted the crucified to be taken down and buried. We find in the summary of Roman law, known as the *Digesta*, the following concessions:

The bodies of those who are condemned to death should not be refused their relatives; and the Divine Augustus, in the Tenth Book of his *Life*, said that this rule had been observed. At present, the bodies of those who have been punished are only buried when this has been requested and permission granted; and sometimes it is not permitted, especially where persons have been convicted of high treason.   (48.24.1)

The bodies of persons who have been punished should be given to whoever requests them for the purpose of burial.   (48.24.3)

The *Digesta* refers to requests to take down bodies of the crucified. Josephus himself makes this request of Titus (*Life* 420–21). Of course, Roman crucifixion often did not permit burial, request or no request. Non-burial was part of the horror – and the deterrent – of crucifixion. But crucifixion – during peacetime – just outside the walls of Jerusalem was another matter. Given Jewish sensitivities and customs, burial would have been expected, even demanded.

The evidence thus far reviewed strongly encourages us to think that in all probability Jesus was indeed buried and that his corpse and those of the two men crucified with him would not have been left hanging on the cross overnight and perhaps indefinitely, or at most cast into a ditch or shallow grave to be exposed to animals. Quite apart from any concerns with the deceased men or their families, the major concern would have had to do with the defilement of the land and the holy city. Politically too it seems unlikely that on the eve of Passover, a holiday that celebrates Israel's liberation from foreign domination, Pilate would have wanted to provoke the Jewish population and incite Jewish nationalism. Moreover it is equally improbable that the ruling priests, who had called for Jesus' death, would have wanted to appear completely indifferent to Jewish sensitivities, either with respect to the dead or with respect to corpse impurity and defilement of the land. It seems most probable that the priests would have raised no objections to the burial of the three men. Indeed they would probably have arranged to have them buried, before nightfall, in tombs reserved for executed criminals, which is what is actually stated in the Mishnah (*m. Sanh.* 6.5–6) and, with respect to Jesus, in the Gospels.

The burial of Jesus

One hundred years ago Kirsopp Lake argued that the followers of Jesus knew that their master had been buried; they just didn't know where. Lake famously proposed what has become known as the Wrong Tomb theory, in which the story of the resurrection of Jesus is explained away. According to this theory, we are to believe that the women who looked on as the body of Jesus was placed in a criminal's tomb returned the following Sunday morning to a similar but wrong tomb. Finding it unoccupied and misunderstanding the words of a helpful young man (proposed to be 'He is not here; he is up there'), the frightened and confused women ran away and told the disciples about their strange experience. From this report the disciples concluded that Jesus must have been raised from the dead. How the followers of Jesus could be so inept and gullible is not explained.

Other intriguing alternative theories have also been proposed. One is dubbed the Swoon Theory, whereby it is suggested that a wounded and comatose Jesus was placed in a tomb, a few days later awakened, somehow extricated himself and then found his way to his startled disciples, creating in them the impression that he had been resurrected and glorified. Why his disciples would have viewed a seriously injured, limping Jesus in such terms is not clear. And, of course, we have been taxed with a series of conspiracy theories, from Hugh Schonfield's *The Passover Plot* to Michael Baigent's silly *The Jesus Papers*.

All of these alternative theories stumble over archaeological and literary evidence, mostly having to do with Jewish burial traditions. Suggestions that Jesus' followers would not be able to find the correct tomb in which their master had been interred or that a still living Jesus would be buried and then, awakening, could actually manage to exit the tomb and be perceived by anyone in any way other than what he was – a badly injured man in need of medical attention – have not impressed qualified historians and archaeologists. The conspiracy theories are even more ludicrous, not only unable to explain how it is that such a grotesque secret was kept by so many, but also unable to discover a cogent motive for such a caper in the first place.

It is estimated that the necropolis surrounding Jerusalem – mostly to the north, east and south of the city – is made up of some 800 tombs, some two dozen of which can be classified as monumental tombs and mausolea.[9] Several impressive examples of such tombs run the length of the Kidron Valley, at the base of Mount Scopus, northeast of the Old City and at the base of the Mount of Olives, opposite the eastern side of the Temple Mount (Figure 5.4).

Our survey begins with the so-called Tomb of Simon the Just, about one kilometre north of the Old City, a short distance from the Nablus Road. The tomb is named after Simon the high priest (d. 196 BCE), who is celebrated in the Wisdom of Yeshua ben Sira (Sir. 50.1–21; 'Abot 1.2). However, the tomb actually belonged to one Julia Sabine, from the beginnings of the Common Era, as indicated by an inscription. Although this tomb is of little architectural significance, its ancient tradition of Jewish pilgrimage is important. As one walks south through the Kidron Valley one can view the so-called Tomb (or Pillar) of Absalom, an unusual mausoleum that dates to the first century CE and stands some 20 metres high, eclectically ornamented with Ionic columns, a Doric frieze and an Egyptian cornice. The structure is crowned with a concave conical roof, its most distinctive feature. It gains the name 'Pillar of Absalom' from 2 Samuel 18.18:

> Now Absalom in his lifetime had taken and set up for himself the pillar, which is in the King's Valley, for he said, 'I have no son to keep my name in remembrance'; he called the pillar after his own name, and it is called 'Absalom's pillar' to this day.

Tucked behind and to the northeast of the Tomb of Absalom is the Tomb (or Cave) of Jehoshaphat, another misnamed tomb. The tomb comprises eight chambers, whose entrance is supported by two square pillars. Built later (perhaps early in the first century CE), the Tomb of Jehoshaphat belonged to the same family who owned the Tomb of Absalom. Its gabled facade will be discussed on page 146.

Moving south, one next encounters the Tomb of the Sons of Hezir, a priestly family, which dates to the first or second century BCE and whose entrance is adorned with two Doric columns. After the Hezir tomb comes the so-called Tomb of Zechariah, with its Ionic pilasters and pyramid-shaped top. The tomb is covered with small, neatly incised Hebrew inscriptions, and probably dates to the first century BCE. Next comes the so-called Tomb of Pharaoh's Daughter. The tomb is east of Ophel and north of the Silwan Village and is one of several very early tombs. Monolithic, at one time it too was adorned

Figure 5.4 Tombs in the Kidron Valley
In the Kidron Valley, at the foot of the Mount of Olives, one finds (from left to right) the Tomb of Absalom, the Tomb of the Sons of Hezir and the Tomb of Zechariah (with the distinctive pyramid roof).

by a pyramid top. It contains a burial chamber and gabled ceiling. Immediately south is a second monolithic tomb sometimes called the Tomb of the Royal Steward. The facade was removed by Charles Clermont-Ganneau in 1870 and is now in the British Museum. Part of a fragmentary inscription reads 'yahu who is over the house'. Adjacent are the remains of another monolithic tomb.

Where the Kidron and Hinnom valleys intersect one finds the Akeldama tombs. Several of these are of the highest quality, judging by the interior architecture, artistic touches and adorned ossuaries. One may have belonged to the family of Annas, high priest 9–15 CE (Josephus, *Ant.* 20.198; Luke 3.2; John 18.13; Acts 4.6). It is palatial in size, design and ornamentation, and at one time was adorned with an impressive superstructure. The quality of this tomb complex and its location – remnants of the siege wall mentioned by Josephus are nearby; *J.W.* 5.506 – support the identification.

Moving west and then north along the Hinnom Valley one approaches the area in which is found the Tomb of Herod's Family. The tomb, discovered in 1892, is about one-third of a kilometre due west of the southwest corner of the wall of the Old City, not far from the modern King David Hotel, on the site of the Nicophoria Monastery. The tomb's superstructure is long gone but the crypt is beautifully decorated and contained several decorated sarcophagi. Its distinctive feature is the large wheel-shaped stone that served as the door to the vault.

Another half kilometre west one comes to the Tomb of Jason, which was discovered in 1956 in Rehavia (or Rehov), western Jerusalem. It is supported by a single pillar instead of the traditional two, and is topped with a pyramid. Along with a Greek inscription and several Aramaic inscriptions, charcoal drawings of ships were found scrawled on the walls of the crypt. Coins and pottery found in the crypt date the earliest use of the tomb to the beginning of the first century BCE, continuing to the beginning of the first century CE.

Due north of the Old City one comes to the Tomb of Queen Helena of Adiabene, daughter of Izates the proselyte (Josephus, *J.W.* 5.147). (The tomb is also called, mistakenly, the Tombs of the Kings.) It is by far the largest and most impressive tomb in Jerusalem. A staircase leads down through an arch and into an expansive garden area. The broad opening included a facade 27 metres wide, supported by two large pillars. The queen and two members of her family were interred in this tomb some time after 50 CE. When excavated the tomb contained several decorated sarcophagi. On one of them were inscribed the words 'Queen Saddan'. According to Josephus (*Ant.* 20.95) her tomb was adorned with three pyramids (though their location and relation to Helena's tomb are disputed), possibly one for herself and one for each of her two sons. Supposedly Louis Félicien de Saulcy in 1865 entered the tomb and found an inscription in Aramaic or Palmyrene that included the title and name 'Helena the Queen'. There is no trace of this inscription today.

The Frieze Tomb, located one and a half kilometres north of the Old City, is marked with an ornate facade with a Doric frieze – hence the tomb's name – supported by two pillars. The frieze, topped by a decorated Corinthian cornice, boasts four artistic rosettes. Some 250 metres to the northwest one comes to the so-called Two-Storeyed Tomb or Pilaster Tomb, first excavated by Kurt Galling. As its name implies, this tomb consists of two storeys, originally presenting either a gabled or flat roofline. Parts of the upper storey, along with a Doric frieze, have survived. Hachlili draws attention to the artistic and architectural links between this tomb and some of the Petra tombs.

Another 300 metres or so to the northwest one comes upon the Tomb of Pillars or the Two-Columned Tomb. It originally boasted two columns (one is now lost), a porch, a central chamber and three rooms. It is similar to the Two-Storeyed Tomb. Immediately to the north one comes to the so-called Sanhedrin Tombs. Among this cluster of ornate tombs, one boasts a beautiful gabled facade, large central hall and several burial chambers, with staircases leading to various levels.

About 100 metres to the east of the Sanhedrin Tombs complex is the so-called Tomb of the Grapes, which derives its name from the sculpted grape clusters that adorn the tympanum above the entrance. Centred in the tympanum, just below the point of the gabled top, is an ornate rosette. About half a kilometre north one comes to the Tomb of Umm el-ʿAmmed (in Nahal Zofim). The Cave of Umm el-ʿAmmed (named after the wadi in which it is located) was decorated with a facade and possessed two chambers with burial niches. The ornate cornice is supported by two columns and two pilasters.

A short distance south of Hebrew University on Mount Scopus one comes to the Tomb of the Hermit and the Tomb of Nicanor. The Tomb of Nicanor was discovered on Mount Scopus in 1902. This large tomb, dating to the first century CE and possessing four branches of burial chambers, contained several decorated ossuaries, including an important inscription that reads: 'The bones of the [sons] of Nicanor the Alexandrian who made the doors. Nicanor Alexa.'

Observation of the monumental tombs, especially those that run along the Kidron Valley, clarifies Jesus' scathing remarks against his critics: 'You are like whitewashed tombs'; and 'You build the tombs of the prophets!' (Matt. 23.27, 29). At the approach of major festivals these tombs were whitewashed and sometimes the inscriptions were highlighted with bright colours. Jesus' graphic comparisons would have readily conjured up familiar images in the minds of his hearers.

Summing up

The literary, historical and archaeological evidence points in one direction: the body of Jesus was placed in a tomb, according to Jewish custom. Furthermore, there is no good reason to think that family and friends of Jesus had no idea where he was buried or had no plans eventually to recover his skeletal remains and transfer them to his family tomb or to another place of honour.

In view of the evidence, I believe the burial narratives of the Gospels deserve a fair reading. If their respective reports are coherent and if they accord with known literary and archaeological evidence, then they should be accepted.[10] In my opinion much of the scepticism that has been voiced is not particularly critical and often reflects ignorance of the Jewish burial traditions that this chapter has taken pains to review.

The Gospels tell us that 'Pilate . . . granted the body to Joseph', who 'laid it in a tomb' (Mark 15.42–46). According to Jewish law and custom the executed criminal could not be buried in his family tomb. Instead his body was to be placed in one of the burial vaults set aside for such persons (*m. Sanh.* 6.5–6; *Semahot* 13.7). There it had to remain until the flesh had decomposed. One rabbinic text addresses this point, specifically in reference to someone who has been crucified: 'If one's [relative] has been crucified in his city, one should not continue to reside there . . . Until when is one so forbidden? Until the flesh is completely decomposed and the identity unrecognizable from the bones' (*Semahot* 2.13). Because the Jewish Council (or Sanhedrin) delivered Jesus to the Roman authorities for execution, it was incumbent upon it to arrange for proper burial (as in *m. Sanh.* 6.5 cited above). This task fell to Joseph of Arimathea, a member of the Council. There is, to be sure, apologetic at work. But try as they might, the evangelists cannot remove the shame of Jesus' death as a criminal and the legal requirement that forbids the burial of his body in a place of honour.[11] The Gospel narrative, including the story of the burial under Joseph's supervision, is completely in step with Jewish practice, which Roman authorities respected during peacetime.

The Gospels tell us that 'Mary Magdalene and Mary the mother of Joses saw where the body was laid' (Mark 15.47). It was necessary for Jesus' family and friends to observe the place where his body was placed, for it was not placed in a tomb that belonged to his family or was otherwise under their control. The reburial of the bones of Yehohanan, the man who also had been crucified under the authority of Pontius Pilate, demonstrates that the Jewish people knew how to note and remember the place of primary burial. The family and friends of Jesus anticipated recovering his skeletal remains, perhaps one year later, so that they 'may be transferred from a wretched place to an honoured place', as the law allowed (*Semahot* 13.7; *m. Sanh.* 6.6).

Jesus was placed in the tomb on Friday afternoon. The first opportunity for anyone to visit the tomb, during daylight hours, was Sunday morning. The Gospels tell us that 'Mary Magdalene, and Mary the mother of James, and Salome bought spices, so that they might go and anoint him. And very early on the first day of the week, when the sun had risen, they went to the tomb' (Mark 16.1b–2). The women's intention to anoint the body indicates their intention to mourn for their master in the tomb itself. In the cases of executed criminals, *private* mourning was allowed. As has already been mentioned, the spices were to be used to perfume the corpse to mask the unpleasant odour.

As the women approach the tomb, they ask: 'Who will roll away the stone?' (Mark 16.3). Matthew says a guard was posted, to prevent the removal of Jesus' body (Matt. 27.65–66). We should probably assume that the evangelist is referring to the custodian, whose placement in the vicinity of the tombs set aside for executed criminals was to see that burial laws were not violated. The most serious of these laws was the prohibition against moving a body from a place of dishonour to a place of honour (see Figure 5.5). The guard or custodian would also enforce the prohibition against public mourning for an executed criminal.

In view of Jesus' status as a criminal and in view of the presence of a guard (perhaps reinforced because of the popularity of Jesus), the women knew that there would be reluctance to assist them in rolling back the stone that covered the opening of Jesus' tomb. They also knew that even their combined strength probably wouldn't be sufficient to roll it aside. Study of the skeletal remains from this period indicates that the average woman was barely

Figure 5.5 Nazareth Inscription
The famous 'Nazareth Inscription', an edict of Caesar forbidding vandalizing or tampering with tombs, including the unlawful removal of a corpse. The inscription is now housed in the Médailles et Antiques de la Bibliothèque Nationale de France. From Franz Cumont, 'Un rescrit impérial sur la violation de sépulture', *Revue Historique* 163 (1930), pp. 341–66; public domain.

150 cm tall and often weighed less than 45 kg. The average man was about 160 cm tall and weighed about 60 kg. Sealing stones weighed 200 kg or more. Even round stones, which were designed to be rolled aside, would have been very difficult to move. The Markan evangelist, moreover, comments that the stone was very large (Mark 16.4b). Accordingly, the women wonder where they might find assistance. Two of the best-known Jerusalem tombs with circular sealing stones and grooved tracks are the Tomb of the Family of Herod and the Garden Tomb (also known as Gordon's Tomb).

According to the Gospels, when the women arrived at the tomb 'they saw that the stone . . . was rolled back' (Mark 16.4). The statement that the 'stone was rolled back' implies a round stone over the entrance to the tomb. In Jewish Palestine of late antiquity at least 90 per cent of the doors were square; fewer than 10 per cent were round. Discovery of the opened and empty tomb would have dismayed the women, especially Mary, the mother of Jesus, when reported to her. For this would mean that the body of Jesus had apparently been relocated. Because Jesus had died on Friday, Sunday was the third day of death, and according to Jewish tradition the face of the corpse was no longer recognizable on the fourth day, as noted above. Therefore the women knew that if Jesus' body was not found *that day*, then it probably would never be identified and therefore could not be claimed and transferred to his family tomb at some future date. Their interpretation of what they saw that Sunday morning was informed by Jewish burial customs, not an expectation of Jesus' resurrection.

When all pertinent data are taken into account we have every reason to conclude that Jesus was properly buried the very day of his death. He was taken down from the cross before nightfall and was buried according to Jewish customs (Mark 15.42—16.4; 1 Cor. 15.4). Put to death as a criminal, he was buried accordingly (*m. Sanh.* 6.5; *Semahot* 13.7). The novel suggestions that perhaps Jesus was left on the cross, unburied (as often was the case outside Israel; Suetonius, *Augustus* 13.1—2; Petronius, *Satyricon* 111), or that his corpse was thrown into a ditch, covered with lime and left for animals to maul, are wholly implausible. Obligation to bury the dead properly, before sundown, to avoid defiling their sacred land, was keenly felt by Jews of late antiquity. The Gospel narratives are plausible and exhibit verisimilitude (which was discussed in the Introduction). In the words of archaeologist Jodi Magness, 'the Gospel accounts describing Jesus' removal from the cross and burial are consistent with archaeological evidence and with Jewish law'.[12]

It is further concluded that it is very probable that some of Jesus' followers – such as the women mentioned in the Gospel accounts – knew where his body had been placed and intended to mark the location, perfume his body and mourn, in keeping with

Jewish customs. The intention was to take possession of Jesus' remains at some point in the future and transfer them to his family burial place. The discovery of the opened tomb and the absence of his body threw the women into confusion and set the stage for a surprising and completely unexpected experience.

Summing up

Archaeology is principally concerned with the recovery and study of human material culture. A find might be no more than a single coin or piece of pottery; a find might be a city. Whatever it is, the archaeologist uncovers it so that it might be studied alongside written texts that have survived from the past.

The ideal is to have access to both artefact and text, and that is usually what we have in the study of the Mediterranean world of late antiquity. We have four first-century Gospels that tell us about Jesus of Nazareth and a number of other figures; we have a number of other first- and second-century documents that provide additional information. Every major city mentioned in the Gospels and Acts has been excavated; so have several villages. We have recovered a number of amazing inscriptions, including one that mentions Pilate, the Roman authority who condemned Jesus to the cross, and another one inscribed on a burial box that may be the name of the Jewish high priest Caiaphas, who interviewed Jesus.

The chapters of this book have attempted to place Jesus and the Gospel narratives into a more detailed context, in the light of archaeological excavations and the material culture these have uncovered. Chapter 1 reviewed the findings of some 40 years of work at Sepphoris. Sepphoris was an impressive Greco-Roman-style city, but in the time of Jesus it was thoroughly Jewish in religious faith and practice. There is no literary and archaeological basis for the proposal that Jesus was influenced by a Cynic presence in Sepphoris or anywhere else in Galilee. The proximity of this city to the village of Nazareth, where Jesus grew up, and the presence of a number of major highways, cautions against the assumption that Jesus and his fellow Galileans were placebound and unacquainted with the larger world.

Chapter 2 reviewed the literary, inscriptional and archaeological evidence for the existence of recognizable synagogue buildings in the time of Jesus. The evidence was seen to be substantial. Of more importance was the acquisition of a better understanding of the role and centrality of this place of gathering for socializing, worship and study. The evidence supports the view that village synagogues played an important part in Jesus' upbringing and development and continued to play an essential, even strategic part in his itinerant preaching and ministry.

Chapter 3 looked into the complicated question of literacy in the time of Jesus and, particularly, into the literacy of Jesus himself. We have seen that literacy throughout the Roman world may have been somewhat higher than estimates a few decades ago. It was also argued, on the grounds of context primarily, that it is probable that Jesus was literate, but not in a scribal or professional sense. Along the way it was also noted that books, because of their intrinsic value and the durable materials from which they were made, were in use for long periods of time, even centuries. It was also observed that private individuals as well as groups promoted literacy and developed libraries for personal and group reading and study.

Chapter 4 reviewed the archaeological findings that shed light on those who competed with and opposed Jesus, particularly the ruling priests. Excavations of portions of the massive Temple Mount complex have been revealing, not least of Herod the Great's ambitions and grandiose self-image. But a number of inscriptions, ornate and monumental funerary architecture, and ruins of what at one time were magnificent mansions give us insight into the world that Jesus confronted when he entered Jerusalem to celebrate Passover with his disciples.

Chapter 5 brought us to a close on a rather grim note by inquiring into what archaeological discoveries have taught us about death in the world of Jesus. Examination of human skeletal remains has revealed just how fragile and short life was in late antiquity. This sober fact also clarifies why it was that crowds pursued Jesus and followed him with enthusiasm. It also cautions the critical scholar not to marginalize the mighty works of Jesus as though these activities were not central to his principal message. The chapter concluded that the Gospel narratives of the death and burial of Jesus are fully in step with literary and archaeological evidence. It is highly probable that Jesus was buried – though not with honour – and that some of his friends and family knew where. Discussion of the resurrection proclamation must take this datum into account.

Interested readers may like to examine some of the books under Suggestions for Further Reading. As I said at the beginning, I do hope you have enjoyed learning about the archaeological discoveries that clarify many aspects of the life of Jesus.

Appendix 1
Have we found the family tomb of Jesus?

The claim made in 2007 that a tomb in East Talpiot, located between Jerusalem and Bethlehem, was the tomb of Jesus and his family throws the discussion of the burial and resurrection of Jesus into a whole new light. The proponents of this view have no doubts that Jesus was properly buried and that he really was dead when he was buried. What is remarkable is that they believe the family tomb of Jesus and the very ossuary that at one time contained his skeletal remains have been found and that there is evidence that Jesus was married and had a son. Can archaeology and related studies shed any light on these remarkable claims?

During construction of town houses in March 1980, two tombs were discovered quite by chance. One of them was hastily excavated and studied by veteran archaeologists Yosef Gat and Amos Kloner, assisted by graduate student Shimon Gibson, who sketched the floor plan. Both tombs were then sealed up and construction continued. The tomb that was examined – in close proximity to what is now 273 Dov Gruner Street – had a rectangular, recessed opening, a square main room and six niches (two in the wall on the right, two in the wall at the back and two in the wall on the left). The square stone that originally covered the entrance was missing and skulls and bone fragments and other debris were scattered about. The tomb had been vandalized in antiquity. Ten ossuaries were recovered, though the actual number of skeletons could not be determined. Gat and Kloner guessed 17. Above the entrance of the tomb is a prominent excised pointed gable with a circle beneath it (Figure A1.1).

A brief report of the discovery and excavation was published by Gat in Hebrew in 1981. Unfortunately Gat died before publishing a longer, more detailed report. Sixteen years after the excavation Amos Kloner published an English report.[1] In 1996 a BBC documentary explored the possibility that the East Talpiot tomb may have had something to do with Jesus and his family. This was explored because of the discovery of the names Jesus, Joseph, Mary, Joseh, Judah and possibly Matthew inscribed on the ossuaries. The documentary generated little interest among scholars and the topic faded away.

In February 2007 Simcha Jacobovici, host and producer of the Canadian television programme *The Naked Archaeologist*, announced, along with writer Charles Pellegrino and movie producer and director

Figure A1.1 Tomb, Talpiot
The entrance and facade of a tomb located in East Talpiot and accidently
unearthed in March 1980. The tomb was examined by Amos Kloner and
Yosef Gat. The theory that this tomb belonged to the family of Jesus has little
to commend it and has been almost universally rejected. Photograph courtesy
of Amos Kloner.

James Cameron, that a tomb in East Talpiot, south Jerusalem, may well
have been the tomb of Jesus of Nazareth and his family.[2] To reach this
conclusion Jacobovici and Pellegrino make several claims, most of which
have serious problems. They resurrect the observation about how most
of the names inscribed on the ossuaries match the names of members
of Jesus' family or circle of disciples, and argue that an X-mark in front of
the inscription 'Yeshua, son of Yehosef' (or 'Jesus, son of Joseph') is a cross,
while the pointed gable and circle ornamentation over the entrance to the
tomb is a secret Christian symbol that identifies the tomb as the tomb of
Jesus and his family.

All of these claims are problematic. Here I can treat two of them,
both having to do with questions of symbolism: first, the claim that
the X-mark at the beginning of the ossuary inscription 'Yeshua, son of
Yehosef' signifies a cross and as such is a Christian symbol; and second,
the claim that the gable and circle excision above the tomb's entrance is
a Jewish-Christian symbol. Both of these claims are quite dubious if not

demonstrably false. No qualified archaeologist agrees with Jacobovici and Pellegrino.

The much-talked-about X-mark on the end of the 'Jesus, son of Joseph' ossuary is not a cross. It is not a symbol of anything, rather it is a stone-mason's mark indicating which end of the lid goes with which end of the box. Because lids were heavy and because these hand-made ossuaries are not symmetrical, the person struggling with the lid would like to know which end goes with which end. The stonemason's mark, usually an X, though sometimes an upside down V (similar to a pointed gable) or an asterisk (*), was etched into one end of the box and at one end (or under-side) of the lid. In the case of the 'Jesus, son of Joseph' ossuary, these facts are clearly noted in Levi Rahmani's *Catalogue of Jewish Ossuaries*,[3] a work known to Jacobovici. Jacobovici's suggestion that the X-mark is a Christian symbol is false and misleading. It is inexcusable.

Perhaps the most demonstrably false claim in the East Talpiot tomb hypothesis is the assertion that the pointed gable with circle over the tomb's entrance is an early Jewish-Christian symbol, which is said to lend import-ant support to the claim that the tomb really did belong to the family of the founder of the Christian movement.[4] This interpretation of the pointed gable and circle symbol is completely erroneous. On the contrary, this symbol suggests that the occupants of the tomb were in all probability numbered among the very people Jesus offended; people who would have called for his death.

The pointed gable over a circle or rosette is seen in other tombs and ossuaries, some of which predate the Christian era and none of which is believed to have anything to do with Jesus and his movement. We see this artistic design in the outer and inner facades of the so-called Sanhedrin Tombs in Jerusalem. Over the inner entrance of this tomb complex one can see the pointed gable over a rosette, comprising acanthus leaves. A gable is also found over the outer entrance, but without rosette. This pattern is seen in the Hinnom Valley Tomb, the Tomb of Jehoshaphat and the so-called Grape Tomb. It is to some of these tombs that Jesus probably alluded when he criticized some of the religious leaders, calling them 'whitewashed sepulchres' – outer appearance beautiful but within are bones and corruption (Matt. 23.27).

In various books concerned with archaeology and Jewish symbols one can find several photographs and facsimiles that depict the gable and circle or rosette. Among the items showing these are ossuaries, a tomb facade, a coin (struck by Philip, tetrarch of Gaulanitis in the time of Jesus) and epitaph art. One of the more common features is the Torah Ark (which contains Scripture scrolls), over which the pointed gable and circle appear.

Scholars have remarked that Jewish funerary art often incorporated imagery influenced by the Herodian temple, and often depicted with pointed gable and circle or rosette.[5] Excavations of the Jewish tombs of Beth Shearim in Galilee have uncovered the same artistic motifs. Again we find a Torah Ark, at the top of which is the gable above a circle (or rosette), painted on a sealing stone.

The gable and circle or rosette pattern is found on several ossuaries, with the circle or rosette on the end of the ossuary, over which rests the gabled lid, or on the end of the lid itself, thus forming the very pattern seen over the entrance to the East Talpiot tomb. An ossuary found on Mount Scopus is particularly relevant, for it depicts monumental facades, with temple motifs, on all four sides. Both ends and one side present pointed gables over entrances. Beneath two of these pointed gables – on one end of the ossuary and on the less-finished side of the ossuary – is a circle, in a pattern quite like what we see over the entrance to the East Talpiot tomb.

And finally, depictions of the Torah Ark, complete with gable and circle (or rosette) are found in synagogue art. Striking examples are found in the art adorning the walls of the Dura Europos Synagogue, where the designs are in reference to the Jerusalem temple.

The evidence is overwhelming, and what has been surveyed above is but a sampling. The conclusion that should be drawn is quite clear: the pointed gable and circle over the entrance to the East Talpiot tomb is Jewish and has nothing to do with Jesus and early Christians. The symbol is probably in reference to the temple. Given the fact that aristocratic and high priestly families were buried in the greater Talpiot area (among them possibly the family of Caiaphas, former high priest), and the fact that every single name in the East Talpiot tomb is Hasmonean,[6] it is probable that this tomb belonged to a wealthy, aristocratic Jerusalem family with ties to the Jerusalem temple. Indeed, some of the members of the family buried in it may have been ruling priests. The suggestion that the gable and circle adornment over it constituted an early Christian symbol has no foundation and ignores a mountain of contrary evidence.

The proponents of this theory are correct in thinking that Jesus' body would have been buried, in keeping with Jewish customs. But they are completely mistaken in thinking his bones and ossuary, along with those of other members of his family, would have been placed in a high-quality tomb, in the neighbourhood of other tombs containing the remains of aristocratic Jews, adorned with a symbol proclaiming temple and priestly affiliation. Accordingly, it is highly improbable that the East Talpiot tomb had anything to do with Jesus, his family or his movement.[7]

Appendix 2
What did Jesus look like?

For almost two millennia, artists have tried to imagine what Jesus looked like. We have countless portraits of his face and of various scenes from his infancy, childhood, public ministry, death, burial and resurrection. There are post-New Testament era descriptions of Jesus, both as a boy and as an adult. But no one really knows what he looked like, for the simple reason that our earliest sources that describe his activities and record his teachings provide no details. We're not told the colour of his hair, his eyes or what was his height or weight. Was he right- or left-handed? Was there anything distinctive about his walk or mannerisms? Did he have any favourite foods? Or songs? Apart from his family and disciples, did he have any friends? We're told none of these things.

As we ponder these questions we realize that we know little about Jesus apart from his provocative teaching and even more provocative deeds. During the mysterious episode of the transfiguration, the evangelist Mark tells us that Jesus 'was transfigured before them' (Mark 9.3). Matthew adds that the face of Jesus 'shone like the sun' (Matt. 17.2), while Luke says 'the appearance of his face was altered' (Luke 9.29). That's not much to go on. The evangelists tell us more about Jesus' clothes ('glistening, intensely white', 'white as light', 'dazzling white') than they do about Jesus himself.

Recently scientists have tried to 'reconstruct' the face of Jesus. Computer technology and the application of clay to a male skull from antiquity yielded the portrait of a rather nondescript Middle Eastern male[1] (Figure A2.1).

The reconstruction is interesting, but in my opinion hardly necessary. I say this because approximately 900 mummy portraits have been recovered from Egypt of the Greco-Roman period (mostly first to third century CE).[2] The Egyptians and Jews of this period were genetically close. And in fact many Jews travelled to and from Egypt and many lived there. These portraits probably tell us what Jews looked like.

The mummy portraits are in colour and many exhibit remarkable detail and realism (see Figures A2.2 and A2.3). Facial reconstructions – along the lines of what was done to 'reconstruct Jesus' – often match the funeral portrait surprisingly closely. Thus the science corroborates the accuracy of the artwork and the artwork gives us confidence in the science.

Men are usually bearded (lightly, not heavily), with dark, full eyebrows and thick curly hair. The hair is almost always dark brown, almost black.

Figure A2.1 The face of Jesus?
An artistic/scientific 'reconstruction' of the face of Jesus. Photograph courtesy of the BBC.

The clothing very much exhibits Greco-Roman style, usually suggesting high standing economically and socially, which is consistent with possessing the wherewithal to commission the mummy portraits in the first place. If the clothing were altered to match typically Jewish clothing, which will be discussed shortly, we would probably have before us close approximations of what Jewish males looked like in the first two or three centuries of the Common Era.

Women and teenaged girls are usually portrayed in stylish apparel. Again the Roman influence is obvious. Makeup can be detected in some cases. Mature women are wearing upmarket tunics and are often adorned with jewellery – earrings, necklaces, tiaras made of flowers or precious metals and gems. Their hair is also made up and will strike people today as rather contemporary. Like men, the women's hair is dark brown. Their eyes are either dark or light brown (almost amber-like in some cases).

Figure A2.2 Berlin Man
The death portrait of a young man (Egypt, c. first century).
Photograph courtesy of Ginny Evans.

Figure A2.3 Berlin Boy
The death portrait of a young boy (Egypt, c. first century).
Photograph courtesy of Ginny Evans.

These mummy portraits – again allowing for differences in dress, jewellery and hair styles – give us a pretty good idea of what Jesus and his Jewish contemporaries looked like. Because Jewish law prohibited the making of human and animal images (Exod. 20.4; Deut. 5.8), Jewish funerary portraits or death masks are relatively rare. Nevertheless, from the non-Jewish mummy portraits it is not hard to imagine the general appearance of Jesus and his disciples, the sisters Mary and Martha or the dying daughter of Jairus the synagogue ruler.[3]

According to Matthew, Mark and Luke, when Jesus was crucified the soldiers 'divided his garments among them by casting lots' (Matt. 27.35; Mark 15.24; Luke 23.34). But John tells the story a bit differently:

> When the soldiers had crucified Jesus they took his garments and made four parts, one for each soldier; also his tunic. But the tunic was without seam, woven from top to bottom; so they said to one another, 'Let us not tear it, but cast lots for it to see whose it shall be.'   (John 19.23–24a)

The statement that the tunic of Jesus 'was without seam, woven from top to bottom', as well as the soldiers' desire not to tear it, seems to imply that a seamless tunic is in some way special. As it turns out, it is. Most tunics were made of two rectangular sheets, sewn together at the top and the sides, with slits for the neck and arms. Examples of this type of tunic, which in the Mishnah is called a *haluq* (literally 'divided'; *m. Nega'im* 11.9), were found in the Bar Kokhba Caves of Nahal Hever, excavated by Yigael Yadin in the early 1960s. Besides the tunics, a child's linen shirt was also found. No fewer than 34 varieties of colours and dyes have been identified in the study of the textiles (mostly linens and wools) found at Nahal Hever and elsewhere near the Dead Sea.

In addition to the tunics and linen shirt, Yadin and his team found balls of wool dyed purple and partially completed fringes (*zizioth*), which Torah-observant Jewish men wore at the corners of their garments.[4] Because of these finds we can now envisage more accurately Jesus' dress and the story of the woman with the haemorrhage who touches the fringe of his garment, hoping to be made well (Mark 5.28).

Sandals and shoes have been found at Nahal Hever (in the Cave of Letters), Masada, 'Ein-Gedi, Jericho, Nahal Mishmar, Wadi Murabba'at (in Cave 1) and Wadi el-Habibi. The soles of these sandals and shoes are made of layers of leather, fastened with leather thongs or straps. Nails were not used, probably in keeping with the rabbinic prohibition against wearing nail-studded shoes on the sabbath (*m. Šabb.* 6.2; *b. Šabb.* 60a).[5]

Jews may have avoided using nails in the making of their sandals and shoes; the Romans did not. A number of remarkably well-preserved Roman sandals and boots were recovered at Vindolanda, the site of the Roman fort and settlement in Britain discussed in Chapter 3, dating to the end of the first century CE and beginning of the second. The leather soles and straps are fastened with nails and metal fasteners.[6]

From these discoveries we can imagine a composite portrait of Jesus, the general appearance of his face and hair, his clothing, which included fringes – and phylacteries too – and his sandals. It is likely that more affluent Jews, many of them in cities, would have worn clothing of higher quality. It is also probable that this higher quality clothing would have exhibited traits of Roman style, perhaps similar to what we see in the Egyptian mummy portraits. The women who numbered among the followers of Jesus would have resembled the women depicted in the Egyptian mummy portraits, but their apparel would have been more modest and it is not too likely that many, if any, would have been adorned with jewellery.

Jesus and his following, representing mostly Galilean villagers, would not have stood out but would have blended in with the crowds of pilgrims making their way to Jerusalem for the Passover festival. Jesus' seamless tunic perhaps marked his dress as somewhat special, but we cannot be sure. Because no Gospel describes his appearance, we should probably assume there was nothing remarkable about his face, bearing or build. Because we actually know what people in his world looked like and because there is no good reason to think Jesus was different or unusual, there really is no mystery. Jesus probably looked like most 30-year-old Jewish men in the first century, and we have a pretty good idea of how they looked.

Notes

Introduction

1 ON THE CORRELATION OF ARCHAEOLOGY AND BIBLICAL TEXTS See Ronald S. Hendel, 'Giants at Jericho', *BAR* 35/2 (2009), pp. 20, 66; quotation from p. 20.

2 ON THE PRINCIPAL GOAL OF ARCHAEOLOGY Consider carefully Kenneth Holum's comments: 'The point of our work is not to try to prove or disprove the Bible. It is to help scientists understand the ancient cultures.' Holum is a professor of history and archaeology at the University of Maryland. The quotation is from an interview (24 October 1993) and is published in Jeffrey L. Sheler, *Is the Bible True? How Modern Debates and Discoveries Affirm the Essence of the Scriptures* (San Francisco: HarperCollins, 1999), p. 62.

3 ON THE HOUSE OF DAVID INSCRIPTION See Avraham Biran, 'An Aramaic Stele Fragment from Tel Dan', *IEJ* 43 (1993), pp. 81–98; André Lemaire, '"House of David" Restored in Moabite Inscription', *BAR* 20/3 (1994), pp. 30–7; 'The Tel Dan Stela as a Piece of Royal Historiography', *JSOT* 81 (1998), pp. 3–14. For a response to minimalists who tried to discount the inscription, see Anson F. Rainey, 'The "House of David" and the House of the Deconstructionists', *BAR* 20/6 (1994), p. 47.

4 ON THE EVIDENCE FOR A TENTH-CENTURY UNITED MONARCHY OF ISRAEL See Amihai Mazar, 'Archaeology and the Biblical Narrative: The Case of the United Monarchy', in Reinhard G. Kratz and Hermann Spieckermann (eds), *One God – One Cult – One Nation: Archaeological and Biblical Perspectives* (Berlin and New York: de Gruyter, 2010), pp. 29–58.

5 FOR FURTHER DISCUSSION OF THE QEIYAFA OSTRACON See Alan Millard, 'The Ostracon from the Days of David Found at Khirbet Qeiyafa', *Tyndale Bulletin* 62 (2011), pp. 1–13; Stephen J. Andrews, 'The Oldest Attested Hebrew Scriptures and the Khirbet Qeiyafa Inscription', in Craig A. Evans (ed.), *The World of Jesus and the Early Church: Identity and Interpretation in the Early Communities of Faith* (Peabody, MA: Hendrickson, 2011), pp. 153–68.

6 ON THE COLLAPSE OF BIBLICAL MINIMALISM See Yosef Garfinkel, 'The Birth and Death of Biblical Minimalism', *BAR* 37/3 (2011), pp. 46–53, 78. This succinct essay surveys the evidence that has been briefly reviewed here. Garfinkel is the Yigael Yadin Professor of Archaeology

at the Hebrew University in Jerusalem and since 2007 has directed the excavations at Khirbet Qeiyafa.

7 ON THE DEAD SEA SCROLLS AND JESUS See Craig A. Evans, 'Jesus and the Dead Sea Scrolls', in Peter W. Flint and James C. VanderKam (eds), *The Dead Sea Scrolls after Fifty Years: A Comprehensive Assessment*, vol. 2 (Leiden: Brill, 1999), pp. 573–98.

8 FOR THE IDEA THAT JESUS OF NAZARETH WAS NOT A HISTORICAL PERSON See Tom Harpur, *The Pagan Christ: Recovering the Lost Light* (Toronto: Thomas Allen Publishers, 2004).

9 TOM HARPUR As quoted in Ken Gallinger, 'A Truly Spiritual Person Never Stops Thinking about the Implications of the Christos', *United Church Observer* 74/11 (2011), pp. 30–1; quotation from p. 31.

10 FOR REFUTATION OF HARPUR'S PAGAN CHRIST See Stanley E. Porter and Stephen J. Bedard, *Unmasking the Pagan Christ: An Evangelical Response to the Cosmic Christ Idea* (Toronto: Clements, 2006). Porter and Bedard show that Harpur not only misrepresents Christianity and the Gospel accounts of the life, death and resurrection of Jesus, he misrepresents the various religions he contends are Christianity's precursors.

11 ROBERT PRICE See Price's contribution and its refutation in James K. Beilby and Paul R. Eddy (eds), *The Historical Jesus: Five Views* (Downers Grove, IL: InterVarsity Press, 2009), pp. 55–103.

12 ON PAUL'S ACQUAINTANCE WITH THE DISCIPLES OF JESUS See James D. G. Dunn, 'The Relationship between Paul and Jerusalem According to Galatians 1 and 2', *NTS* 28 (1982), pp. 461–78, esp. 463–6; 'Once More – Gal 1.18: ἱστορῆσαι Κηφᾶν in Reply to Otfried Hofius', *ZNW* 76 (1985), pp. 138–9. Dunn understands Paul's ἱστορῆσαι Κηφᾶν as 'to get information from Cephas'. See also G. D. Kilpatrick, 'Galatians 1:18 ἱστορῆσαι Κηφᾶν', in A. J. B. Higgins (ed.), *New Testament Essays: Studies in Memory of Thomas Walter Manson 1893–1958* (Manchester: Manchester University Press, 1959), pp. 144–9. Kilpatrick came to the same conclusion.

13 ON PAPIAS, BISHOP OF HIERAPOLIS See Berthold Altaner, *Patrology* (New York: Herder & Herder, 1960), p. 113; Michael W. Holmes, *The Apostolic Fathers: Greek Texts and English Translations* (3rd edn, Grand Rapids: Baker Academic, 2007), pp. 735–41.

14 ON QUADRATUS THE APOLOGIST See Altaner, *Patrology*, pp. 117–18; Holmes, *The Apostolic Fathers*, pp. 720–1.

15 ON CLEMENT, IGNATIUS AND POLYCARP See Altaner, *Patrology*, pp. 99–111; Holmes, *The Apostolic Fathers*, pp. 33–9, 167–81, 272–9. For more on early Jesus material in *1 Clement*, see Andrew Gregory, '*1 Clement* and the Writings that Later Formed the New Testament', in Andrew

Gregory and Christopher Tuckett (eds), *The Reception of the New Testament in the Apostolic Fathers* (Oxford: Oxford University Press, 2005), pp. 129–57.

16 ON THE AUTHENTICITY OF THE JESUS PASSAGE IN JOSEPHUS See John P. Meier, 'Jesus in Josephus: A Modest Proposal', *CBQ* 52 (1990), pp. 76–103; Steve Mason, *Josephus and the New Testament: Second Edition* (Peabody, MA: Hendrickson, 2003), pp. 225–36. Mason is a respected Josephus scholar.

17 ON THE IMPORTANCE OF VERISIMILITUDE IN HISTORICAL RESEARCH See Louis Gottschalk, 'The Historian and the Historical Document', in Louis Gottschalk, Clyde Kluckhorn and Robert Angell, *The Use of Personal Documents in History, Anthropology and Sociology* (Bulletin 53; New York: Social Science Research Council, 1945), pp. 35–8. Gottschalk equates verisimilitude with credibility. It is to this principle that A. N. Sherwin-White alludes when he says: 'The basic reason for this confidence [in the New Testament Gospels] is, if put summarily, the existence of external confirmations' (*Roman Society and Roman Law in the New Testament: The Sarum Lectures 1960–61* (Oxford: Oxford University Press, 1963), pp. 186–7).

18 ON THE USE OF THE GOSPELS IN ARCHAEOLOGY AND HISTORY See Eric M. Meyers (ed.), *Galilee through the Centuries: Confluence of Cultures* (Duke Judaic Studies 1; Winona Lake, IN: Eisenbrauns, 1999); Sean Freyne, *Galilee and Gospel: Collected Essays* (WUNT 125; Tübingen: Mohr Siebeck, 2000); Mark A. Chancey, *Greco-Roman Culture and the Galilee of Jesus* (SNTSMS 134; Cambridge: Cambridge University Press, 2005); James H. Charlesworth (ed.), *Jesus and Archaeology* (Grand Rapids: Eerdmans, 2006).

1 In the shadow of Sepphoris: growing up in Nazareth

1 FOR A REPORT OF THE EXCAVATION OF THE SACRED GROTTO OF THE BASILICA OF THE ANNUNCIATION See Bellarmino Bagatti, *Excavations in Nazareth: Vol. 1, From the Beginning till the XII Century* (2 vols, Publications of the Studium Biblicum Franciscanum 17; Jerusalem: Franciscan Printing Press, 1969), pp. 174–218.

2 ON THE IDEA THAT JESUS GREW UP IN ISOLATION See Joseph Klausner, *Jesus of Nazareth: His Life, Times and Teaching* (London: George Allen & Unwin, 1925), pp. 236–7. Klausner speaks poetically of Jesus 'cut off by mountains from the great world, wrapped up in natural beauty'. But even in more recent times scholars still speak of Jesus growing up in rural isolation. See E. P. Sanders, 'Jesus: His Religious "Type"', *Reflections* (1992), pp. 4–12. Sanders states that it would have taken Jesus half a day

to walk from Nazareth to Sepphoris. In reality it only takes a little over one hour. Sanders is correct, however, in saying that Jesus was not an 'urbanite' and that he seems to have avoided cities. See E. P. Sanders, *The Historical Figure of Jesus* (London and New York: Penguin, 1993), p. 12.

3 ON THE DISTRIBUTION OF POTTERY IN FIRST-CENTURY GALILEE See James F. Strange, 'The Sayings of Jesus and Archaeology', in James H. Charlesworth and Loren L. Johns (eds), *Hillel and Jesus: Comparisons of Two Major Religious Leaders* (Minneapolis: Fortress, 1997), pp. 291–305, esp. 301–2. The source of pottery can be identified by neutron activation analysis.

4 ON JESUS AS JEWISH CYNIC See John Dominic Crossan, *The Historical Jesus: The Life of a Mediterranean Jewish Peasant* (San Francisco: Harper-Collins, 1991), pp. 421–2; quotation from p. 421.

5 FOR STUDIES BY SCHOLARS WHO FIND THE CYNIC HYPOTHESIS UNCON-VINCING See David E. Aune, 'Jesus and Cynics in First-Century Palestine: Some Critical Considerations', in Charlesworth and Johns (eds), *Hillel and Jesus*, pp. 176–92; Hans Dieter Betz, 'Jesus and the Cynics: Survey and Analysis of a Hypothesis', *JR* 74 (1994), pp. 453–75; Christopher M. Tuckett, 'A Cynic Q?', *Bib* 70 (1989), pp. 349–76; *Q and the History of Early Christianity: Studies on Q* (Edinburgh: T. & T. Clark, 1996), pp. 368–91; Ben Witherington III, *Jesus the Sage: The Pilgrimage of Wisdom* (Minneapolis: Fortress, 1994), pp. 123–43; Craig A. Evans, 'The Misplaced Jesus: Interpreting Jesus in a Judaic Context', in Bruce D. Chilton, Craig A. Evans and Jacob Neusner (eds), *The Missing Jesus: Rabbinic Judaism and the New Testament. New Research Examining the Historical Jesus in the Context of Judaism* (Leiden and Boston: Brill, 2002), pp. 11–39, esp. 14–27.

6 FOR A COLLECTION OF PARALLELS BETWEEN JESUS AND CYNICS See F. Gerald Downing, *Christ and the Cynics: Jesus and Other Radical Preachers in First-Century Tradition* (JSOT Manuals 4; Sheffield: JSOT Press, 1988).

7 ON THE JEWISH CHARACTER OF GALILEE AND SEPPHORIS IN THE TIME OF JESUS See James F. Strange, 'First Century Galilee from Archaeology and from the Texts', in Douglas R. Edwards and C. Thomas McCollough (eds), *Archaeology and the Galilee: Texts and Contexts in the Graeco-Roman and Byzantine Periods* (Atlanta: Scholars Press, 1997), pp. 39–48; Mark A. Chancey, *The Myth of a Gentile Galilee* (SNTSMS 118; Cambridge: Cambridge University Press, 2002); *Greco-Roman Culture and the Galilee of Jesus* (SNTSMS 134; Cambridge: Cambridge University Press, 2005).

8 FOR ARGUMENTS FOR THE EXISTENCE OF THE THEATRE IN THE TIME OF JESUS AND FOR THE ALLUSIONS TO IT THAT HAVE BEEN SUGGESTED See Richard A. Batey, 'Jesus and the Theatre', *NTS* 30 (1984), pp. 563–74; James F. Strange, 'Some Implications of Archaeology for New Testament Studies', in James H. Charlesworth and Walter P. Weaver (eds), *What Has Archaeology To Do with Faith?* (Faith and Scholarship Colloquies; Philadelphia: Trinity Press International, 1992), pp. 23–59, esp. 44–5. Batey, Strange and other archaeologists point to evidence, such as pottery and coins, that supports an early first-century date. See James F. Strange, 'Six Campaigns at Sepphoris: The University of South Florida Excavations, 1983–1989', in Lee I. Levine (ed.), *The Galilee in Late Antiquity* (New York: Jewish Theological Seminary of America, 1992), pp. 339–55, esp. 342–3; Richard A. Batey, 'Did Antipas Build the Sepphoris Theater?', in James H. Charlesworth (ed.), *Jesus and Archaeology* (Grand Rapids: Eerdmans, 2006), pp. 111–19.

9 ON THE WORD *PLATEIA* This word appears in rabbinic literature (*y. Ketub.* 1.10) as a loan word and in fact occurs in reference to the city of Sepphoris, which boasted a theatre. For details see Strange, 'Some Implications of Archaeology', pp. 44 and 57–8, n. 83.

10 ON THE SYNAGOGUE EXCAVATED AT CAPERNAUM See James F. Strange, 'Synagogue Where Jesus Preached Found at Capernaum', *BAR* 9/6 (1983), pp. 24–31. More will be said about this synagogue in Chapter 2.

11 ON THE SO-CALLED HOUSE OF PETER See James F. Strange, 'Has the House where Jesus Stayed in Capernaum Been Found?' *BAR* 8/6 (1982), pp. 26–37.

12 ON THE OFFICER OF CAPERNAUM See John Dominic Crossan and Jonathan Reed, *Excavating Jesus* (San Francisco: HarperCollins, 2001), pp. 87–9. On the second-century dating of the Roman bath, see Jonathan Reed, *Archaeology and the Galilean Jesus: A Re-examination of the Evidence* (Harrisburg, PA: Trinity Press International, 2000), pp. 155–6.

13 ON JESUS, ARCHAEOLOGY AND URBAN LIFE See Strange, 'Some Implications of Archaeology', pp. 41–7.

14 ON SOCIAL, ECONOMIC AND URBAN FACTORS IN FIRST-CENTURY JEWISH PALESTINE See Bruce J. Malina and Richard L. Rohrbaugh, *Social-Science Commentary on the Synoptic Gospels* (Minneapolis: Fortress, 1992); Douglas E. Oakman, *Jesus and the Peasants* (Matrix: The Bible in Mediterranean Context 4; Eugene, OR: Cascade Books, 2007).

15 ON THE SYNAGOGUE OF NAZARETH See Bagatti, *Excavations in Nazareth*, pp. 233–4. The ruins date no earlier than the second century CE. The remains of the first-century synagogue, which may have been little more than a private dwelling, have not been found.

2 Among the devout: religious formation in the synagogue

1 FOR ARGUMENTS THAT THERE WERE NO SYNAGOGUE BUILDINGS PRIOR TO
70 CE See Howard Clark Kee, 'The Transformation of the Synagogue after
70 C.E.: Its Import for Early Christianity', *NTS* 36 (1990), pp. 481–500;
'The Changing Meaning of Synagogue: A Response to Richard Oster',
NTS 40 (1994), pp. 281–3; 'Defining the First-Century CE Synagogue:
Problems and Progress', *NTS* 41 (1995), pp. 481–500; reprinted in Howard
Clark Kee and Lynn H. Cohick (eds), *The Evolution of the Synagogue:
Problems and Progress* (Harrisburg, PA: Trinity Press International, 1999),
pp. 7–26. In the second study, Kee is responding to Richard Oster, whose
study is cited in the following note.

2 FOR ARGUMENTS THAT THERE WERE SYNAGOGUES IN ISRAEL PRIOR
TO 70 CE See Richard E. Oster, 'Supposed Anachronism in Luke–
Acts' Use of συναγωγή: A Rejoinder to H. C. Kee', *NTS* 39 (1993),
pp. 178–208; Rainer Riesner, 'Synagogues in Jerusalem', in Richard
Bauckham (ed.), *The Book of Acts in its Palestinian Setting* (Grand
Rapids: Eerdmans, 1995), pp. 179–211; Lee I. Levine, 'The Nature
and Origin of the Palestine Synagogue Reconsidered', *JBL* 115 (1996),
pp. 425–48; Kenneth Atkinson, 'On Further Defining the First-Century
C.E. Synagogue: Fact or Fiction? A Rejoinder to H. C. Kee', *NTS* 43
(1997), pp. 491–502; John S. Kloppenborg Verbin, 'Dating Theodotos
(*CIJ* 1404)', *JJS* 51 (2000), pp. 243–80; 'The Theodotos Synagogue
Inscription and the Problem of First-Century Synagogue Buildings',
in James H. Charlesworth (ed.), *Jesus and Archaeology* (Grand Rapids:
Eerdmans, 2006), pp. 236–82; Lester L. Grabbe, 'Synagogue and Sanhedrin in the First Century', in Stanley E. Porter and Tom Holmén (eds),
Handbook for the Study of the Historical Jesus (4 vols, Leiden: Brill, 2011),
pp. 2:1723–45, esp. 1723–9. Grabbe rightly remarks that virtually no
one has followed Kee.

3 ON THE NORTH AFRICAN SYNAGOGUE INSCRIPTION See *SEG* XVII 823
(= *CJZ* no. 72). For discussion, see Oster, 'Supposed Anachronism',
p. 187; Kloppenborg Verbin, 'Dating Theodotos', pp. 247–8.

4 ON JEWISH CONNECTIONS BETWEEN CYRENAICA AND JUDEA See
Kloppenborg Verbin, 'Dating Theodotos', p. 248, n. 16.

5 ON THE DISCOVERY OF THE JERUSALEM SYNAGOGUE INSCRIPTION See
Raimund Weill, 'La Cité de David: Compte rendu des fouilles exécutées
à Jérusalem sur le site de la ville primitive. Campaigne de 1913–1914',
REJ 69 (1919), pp. 3–85 + pls, esp. pl. XXVa; 'La Cité de David: Compte
rendu des fouilles exécutées à Jérusalem sur le site de la ville primitive.
Campaigne de 1913–1914', *REJ* 70 (1920), pp. 1–36, esp. 30–4.

6 For a summary of epigraphical analysis of the Theodotos inscription See Kloppenborg Verbin, 'The Theodotos Synagogue Inscription', pp. 266–77.

7 For a summary of the archaeological and contextual factors of the Theodotos inscription See Kloppenborg Verbin, 'The Theodotos Synagogue Inscription', pp. 260–6. Kloppenborg Verbin reasonably concludes that the Theodotos synagogue was built near the turn of the era.

8 For bibliography and brief descriptions of the seven pre-70 ce synagogues of Israel See Kloppenborg Verbin, 'The Theodotos Synagogue Inscription', pp. 248–50 + nn. 39–48; Anders Runesson, Donald D. Binder and Birger Olsson, *The Ancient Synagogue from its Origins to 200 ce: A Source Book* (Leiden: Brill, 2010), pp. 25–76. For a collection of important essays on this topic, see Lee I. Levine (ed.), *Ancient Synagogues Revealed* (Jerusalem: Israel Exploration Society, 1981); and Hanswulf Bloedhorn and Gil Hüttenmeister, 'The Synagogue', in W. Horbury et al. (eds), *The Cambridge History of Judaism, Vol. 3, The Early Roman Period* (Cambridge: Cambridge University Press, 1999), pp. 267–97.

9 On the basalt foundation of the Capernaum synagogue See Michael Avi-Yonah, 'Some Comments on the Capernaum Excavations', in Levine (ed.), *Ancient Synagogues Revealed*, pp. 60–2; Runesson, Binder and Olsson, *The Ancient Synagogue*, pp. 25–32; John Dominic Crossan and Jonathan Reed, *Excavating Jesus* (San Francisco: HarperCollins, 2001), pp. 90–1. Reed rightly comments that to speak of a first-century synagogue at Capernaum is not supported by archaeological evidence, for the evidence at hand is insufficient. I argue for the first-century synagogue, beneath the limestone synagogue, on the basis of Jewish religious tradition and practice.

10 On the excavation of Gamla See Shmaryahu Gutman, 'The Synagogue at Gamla', in Levine (ed.), *Ancient Synagogues Revealed*, pp. 30–4; 'Gamala', *NEAEHL*, pp. 2:459–63; Runesson, Binder and Olsson, *The Ancient Synagogue*, pp. 33–4.

11 On the architectural synagogue 'template' See Z. Maoz, 'The Synagogue of Gamla and the Typology of Second-Temple Synagogues', in Levine (ed.), *Ancient Synagogues Revealed*, pp. 35–41; James F. Strange, 'Archaeology and Ancient Synagogues up to about 200 C.E.', in Alan J. Avery-Peck, Daniel J. Harrington and Jacob Neusner (eds), *When Judaism and Christianity Began: Essays in Memory of Anthony J. Saldarini* (2 vols, JSJSup 85; Leiden: Brill, 2004), pp. 2:483–508.

12 On the excavation of the Herodium See Gideon Foerster, 'Herodium', *NEAEHL*, pp. 2:618–21; Runesson, Binder and Olsson, *The Ancient Synagogue*, pp. 35–6. Tragically Ehud Netzer died in October of 2010 as a result of a fall suffered while working at the Herodium. He was 76. For his assessment of Herod's building activities, including the Herodium, see Ehud Netzer, *The Architecture of Herod, the Great Builder* (TSAJ 117; Tübingen: Mohr Siebeck, 2006).

13 On the excavation of the Jericho synagogue See Ehud Netzer, Ya'akov Kalman and Rachel Laureys, 'A Synagogue from the Hasmonean Period Recently Discovered in the Western Plain of Jericho', *IEJ* 49 (1999), pp. 203–21; Ehud Netzer, 'Jericho', *NEAEHL* Sup. pp. 1798–800; Runesson, Binder and Olsson, *The Ancient Synagogue*, pp. 40–2.

14 For a preliminary report of the Magdala synagogue See Jürgen K. Zangenberg, 'Archaeological News from the Galilee: Tiberias, Magdala and Rural Galilee', *Early Christianity* 1 (2010), pp. 471–84, here 476–7 (includes photograph); J. Corbett, 'New Synagogue Excavations in Israel and Beyond', *BAR* 37/4 (2011), pp. 52–9, esp. 53–6. For discussion of the earlier, erroneous identification of the Magdala synagogue, see Runesson, Binder and Olsson, *The Ancient Synagogue*, p. 55.

15 For a popular account of Yadin's excavation of Masada See Yigael Yadin, *Masada: Herod's Fortress and the Zealots' Last Stand* (New York: Random House, 1966).

16 On the excavation of the Masada synagogue See Yigael Yadin, 'The Synagogue at Masada' and Gideon Foerster, 'The Synagogues at Masada and Herodium', in Levine (ed.), *Ancient Synagogues Revealed*, pp. 19–23 and 24–9 respectively; Ehud Netzer, 'Masada', *NEAEHL*, pp. 3:973–85, esp. 981; Runesson, Binder and Olsson, *The Ancient Synagogue*, pp. 55–7.

17 On the excavation of the Modi'in synagogue See Alexander Onn and Shlomit Weksler-Bdolah, ''Umm el-Umdan, Khirbet (Modi'in)', *NEAEHL* Sup. pp. 2061–3; Runesson, Binder and Olsson, *The Ancient Synagogue*, pp. 57–8.

18 On the excavation of the Qiryat Sefer synagogue See Yitzhak Magen and Yoav Tzionit, 'Qiryat Sefer (Khirbet Badd 'Isa)', *NEAEHL* Sup. pp. 2000–3; Runesson, Binder and Olsson, *The Ancient Synagogue*, pp. 65–6.

19 On the discovery of a synagogue at Shuafat See Abraham Rabinovich, 'Oldest Jewish Prayer Room Discovered on Shuafat Ridge', *Jerusalem Post* (8 April 1991); Runesson, Binder and Olsson, *The Ancient Synagogue*, pp. 75–6.

20 ON THE PURPOSE AND FUNCTION OF FIRST-CENTURY SYNAGOGUES See Moshe Dothan, 'Research on Ancient Synagogues in the Land of Israel', in Benjamin Mazar and Hershel Shanks (eds), *Recent Archaeology in the Land of Israel* (Jerusalem: Israel Exploration Society, 1984), pp. 89–96. See also Yoran Tsafrir, 'The Synagogues at Capernaum and Meroth and the Dating of the Galilean Synagogue', in John H. Humphrey (ed.), *The Roman and Byzantine Near East: Some Recent Archaeological Research* (JRASup 14; Ann Arbor, MI: Journal of Roman Archaeology, 1995), pp. 151–61.

21 ON RABBINIC EVIDENCE OF SYNAGOGUE-BASED SCHOOLS See Shemuel Safrai, 'Education and the Study of Torah', in Shemuel Safrai and Menahem Stern (eds), *The Jewish People in the First Century* (2 vols, CRINT 1.1–2; Assen: Van Gorcum; Philadelphia: Fortress, 1974–6), pp. 2:945–70; quotation from p. 953. For a similar summary of (mostly) rabbinic evidence, see Emil Schürer, *The History of the Jewish People in the Age of Jesus Christ* (3 vols, rev. by Geza Vermes, Fergus Millar and Matthew Black; Edinburgh: T. & T. Clark, 1973–87), pp. 2:415–20; John T. Townsend, 'Education (Greco-Roman)', in *ABD*, pp. 2:312–17, esp. 315–17.

22 ON THE IMPORTANCE OF THE TASSEL IN RABBINIC TRADITION In the Talmud we hear of a pious rabbi, as told by his son: 'On descending a ladder my father stepped on one of the threads and tore it off. He refused to move from the spot until it was replaced' (*b. Šabb.* 188b). Jesus also criticizes the hypocrites for making their phylacteries 'broad'; that is, more obvious. The Gospels do not tell us if Jesus wore phylacteries (leather pouches or bindings that contain verses of Scripture, usually the Shema or related texts). There is no reason to think that he did not. Again, his criticism is not directed against the practice itself; it is directed against ostentation.

23 ON TASSELS IN LATE ANTIQUITY See Yigael Yadin, *Bar-Kokhba: The Rediscovery of the Legendary Hero of the Last Jewish Revolt against Imperial Rome* (London: Weidenfeld & Nicolson, 1971), pp. 83–5. In the Cave of Letters at Nahal Hever, Yadin and his team found a number of partially completed tassels, as well as bundles of wool yarn, dyed blue, from which additional tassels could be made. At Qumran dozens of phylacteries have also been found.

24 ON JESUS AND THE SYNAGOGUE See James D. G. Dunn, 'Did Jesus Attend the Synagogue?' in Charlesworth (ed.), *Jesus and Archaeology*, pp. 206–22. On p. 222 Dunn notes the significance of the tassels on Jesus' clothing.

25 DO THE SCRIBES AND PHARISEES READ OR TEACH? On this question, see Mark Allan Powell, 'Do and Keep What Moses Says (Matthew 23:2–7)',

JBL 114 (1995), pp. 419–35, esp. 431–5. Powell rightly argues that Jesus is not commanding his disciples to observe the *teaching* of the scribes and Pharisees (for their teaching and practice are hypocritical); he is commanding his disciples to obey the *reading* of the law of Moses.

26 ON THE SEAT OF MOSES IN RABBINIC LITERATURE See *Pesiqta deRab Kahana* 1.7: '"The top of the throne was rounded in the back" (1 Kings 10.19) means, according to Rabbi Aha, that the throne resembled the seat of Moses [Hebrew: *qetidra deMosheh*]'; *Exod. Rab.* 43.4 (on Exod. 32.22): Moses 'wrapped himself in his cloak and seated himself in the posture of a sage'; *Song Rab.* 1.3 §1: 'The house of study of Rabbi Eliezer was shaped like an arena, and there was in it a stone which was reserved for him to sit on'; and perhaps *Esth. Rab.* 1.11 (on Esth. 1.2): 'the seat of Israel is a real seat'.

3 In the books: reading, writing and literacy

1 ON THE ILLITERACY OF JESUS See Robert W. Funk and Roy W. Hoover (eds), *The Five Gospels: The Search for the Authentic Words of Jesus* (New York: Macmillan, 1993), p. 27; John Dominic Crossan, *Jesus: A Revolutionary Biography* (New York: HarperCollins, 1994), pp. 25–6; Robert W. Funk, *Honest to Jesus: Jesus for a New Millennium* (San Francisco: HarperCollins, 1996), p. 158; Pieter F. Craffert and Pieter J. J. Botha, 'Why Jesus Could Walk on the Sea but He Could not Read and Write', *Neot* 39 (2005), pp. 5–35. Botha argues for the illiteracy of Jesus in the fourth part of this paper, under the heading 'Was Jesus Literate?' (pp. 21–32). It is to this part of the paper that reference will be made. On the general question of illiteracy in the Mediterranean world of late antiquity, see William V. Harris, *Ancient Literacy* (Cambridge, MA: Harvard University Press, 1989).

2 FOR A SURVEY OF LIBRARIES IN ANTIQUITY See Luciano Canfora, *The Vanished Library: A Wonder of the Ancient World* (London: Hutchinson Radius, 1989).

3 ON LITERACY IN LATE ANTIQUITY Not everyone agrees with the lower rates proposed by Harris and others (see note 1 above). For arguments in support of higher rates of literacy, see Alan Millard, *Reading and Writing in the Time of Jesus* (BibSem 69; Sheffield: Sheffield Academic Press, 2000), esp. pp. 154–84.

4 ON THE WRITING MATERIALS AT QUMRAN See Meir Bar-Ilan, 'Writing Materials', in Lawrence H. Schiffman and James C. VanderKam (eds), *Encyclopedia of the Dead Sea Scrolls* (2 vols, Oxford: Oxford University Press, 2000), pp. 2:996–7.

5 On the scribes and the scriptorium of Qumran See Emanuel Tov, 'Scribal Practices'; 'Scribes'; and Magen Broshi, 'Scriptorium', in Schiffman and VanderKam (eds), *Encyclopedia of the Dead Sea Scrolls*, pp. 2:827–30, 830–1, 831–2 respectively.

6 The portrait of bakery owner Terentius Neo and wife The portrait is housed in the National Archaeological Museum in Naples.

7 The Murecine portrait of Calliope, muse of epic poetry The portrait is housed in the National Archaeological Museum in Naples.

8 For another portrait from Pompeii, featuring a young female, probably single, mimicking Calliope with stylus and *tabulae ceratae* in hand See Alan K. Bowman and J. David Thomas, *The Vindolanda Writing Tablets* (Newcastle upon Tyne: Frank Graham, 1974), p. 29 (pl. XIV).

9 On the Murecine tablets See Judith Harris, *Pompeii Awakened: A Story of Rediscovery* (New York: I. B. Tauris, 2007), pp. 257–8.

10 On the discovery of the wooden writing tablets at Vindolanda See Robin Birley, *Discoveries at Vindolanda* (Newcastle upon Tyne: Frank Graham, 1973); *The Roman Documents from Vindolanda* (Greenhead: Roman Army Museum Publications, 1990); Alan K. Bowman, *Life and Letters on the Roman Frontier: Vindolanda and its People* (London and New York: Routledge, 1998), esp. pp. 13–19.

11 For image of Claudia's invitation to Sulpicia See Bowman, *Life and Letters on the Roman Frontier*, p. 162 (pl. VI).

12 On Claudia's poor penmanship See Alan K. Bowman, 'The Roman Imperial Army: Letters and Literacy on the Northern Frontier', in Alan K. Bowman and Greg Woolf (eds), *Literacy and Power in the Ancient World* (Cambridge and New York: Cambridge University Press, 1994), pp. 109–25; quotations from p. 124.

13 On Vindolanda and the question of literacy See Bowman, 'The Roman Imperial Army', pp. 124–5; *Life and Letters on the Roman Frontier*, pp. 82–99, esp. 83: 'If a literate military establishment appears on the northern frontier of Britain within a decade or two of its occupation by the Romans, then it must have been universal in the Roman provinces.' For important qualifications with respect to low estimations of literacy in the Roman Empire, see Alan K. Bowman, 'Literacy in the Roman Empire: Mass and Mode', in J. H. Humphrey (ed.), *Literacy in the Roman World* (Journal of Roman Archaeology, Supplement Series 3; Ann Arbor, MI: Journal of Roman Archaeology, 1991), pp. 119–31.

14 On the scrolls found in the Villa of Papyri in Herculaneum See Amedeo Maiuri, *Herculaneum and the Villa of the Papyri* (Novara:

Istituto Geografico de Agostini, 1974); Harris, *Pompeii Awakened*, pp. 44–61.

15 ON THE GRAFFITI FOUND IN POMPEII The examples are taken from *Corpus Inscriptionum Latinarum*, vol. 4.

16 ON GRAFFITI IN ISRAEL See Michael E. Stone (ed.), *Rock Inscriptions and Graffiti Project* (3 vols, SBLRBS 28, 29, 31; Atlanta: Scholars Press, 1992–4). Stone and his colleagues catalogued some 8,500 inscriptions and graffiti found in southern Israel: the Judean desert, the desert of the Negev and Sinai. The inscriptions are in several languages, including Hebrew, Aramaic, Greek, Latin, Nabatean, Armenian, Georgian, Egyptian hieroglyphs and others. Not many date to late antiquity, because, unlike the graffiti and inscriptions of Pompeii and Herculaneum, the graffiti and inscriptions in the deserts of Israel were exposed to the eroding elements.

17 ON THE PALATINE GRAFFITO For an early report, see Rodolfo Lanciani, *Ancient Rome in the Light of Recent Discoveries* (Boston: Houghton, Mifflin, 1898), pp. 121–2 + plate. For more recent discussion, see B. Hudson McLean, *An Introduction to Greek Epigraphy of the Hellenistic and Roman Periods* (Ann Arbor: University of Michigan Press, 2002), p. 208 ('discovered in the subterranean chambers of the Roman Palatine Hill'); David L. Balch and Carolyn Osiek, *Early Christian Families in Context: An Interdisciplinary Dialogue* (Grand Rapids: Eerdmans, 2003), pp. 103–4; John Granger Cook, 'Envisioning Crucifixion: Light from Several Inscriptions and the Palatine Graffito', *NovT* 50 (2008), pp. 262–85, esp. 282–5. The original locus of the graffito is disputed. According to Graydon F. Snyder, *Ante Pacem: Archaeological Evidence of Church Life before Constantine* (Macon, GA: Mercer University Press, 1985), pp. 27–8, the graffito was 'found in the servants' quarters of the Imperial Palace'. According to Everett Ferguson, *Backgrounds of Early Christianity* (2nd edn, Grand Rapids: Eerdmans, 1993), pp. 559–61, the graffito was 'scratched on a stone in a guard room on Palatine Hill near the Circus Maximus'.

18 ON THE DATE OF THE PALATINE GRAFFITO See Maria Antonietta Tomei, *Museo Palatino* (Milan: Electa, 1997), pp. 104–5. An image of the graffito is provided on p. 104.

19 CRUCIFIED IN THE MANNER DESCRIBED IN THE *ANTHOLOGIA LATINA* 'The criminal, outstretched on the infamous stake, hopes for escape from his place on the cross' (415.23).

20 ON THE SLAVE THROWING A KISS See Cook, 'Envisioning Crucifixion', p. 283, n. 91.

21 On libraries and collections See George W. Houston, 'Papyrological Evidence for Book Collections and Libraries in the Roman Empire', in William A. Johnson and Holt N. Parker (eds), *Ancient Literacies: The Culture of Reading in Greece and Rome* (Oxford and New York: Oxford University Press, 2009), pp. 233–67. For more on the general topic of collections and archives, see Katelijn Vandorpe, 'Archives and Dossiers', in Roger S. Bagnall (ed.), *The Oxford Handbook of Papyrology* (Oxford: Oxford University Press, 2009), pp. 216–55.

22 On the longevity of Codex Vaticanus See J. Keith Elliott, 'T. C. Skeat on the Dating and Origin of Codex Vaticanus', in T. C. Skeat, *The Collected Biblical Writings of T. C. Skeat* (introduced and edited by J. Keith Elliott; NovTSup 113; Leiden: Brill, 2004), pp. 281–94, here 293.

23 On the longevity of other Christian Bibles Codex Sinaiticus, for example, was corrected in the sixth or seventh century. Codex Ephraemi Rescriptus, produced in the fifth century, was in use for four or five centuries before being overwritten in the twelfth century. See Frederick G. Kenyon, *The Text of the Greek Bible* (3rd edn, ed. A. W. Adams; London: Duckworth, 1975), pp. 41–2, 44. Retired and discarded mss were not corrected; only those still in use.

24 On the tau-rho compendium and its relevance for the style of cross on which Jesus was crucified See Larry W. Hurtado, *The Earliest Christian Artifacts: Manuscript and Christian Origins* (Grand Rapids: Eerdmans, 2006), pp. 147–8.

25 On widespread literacy among the Jewish people See Shemuel Safrai, 'Education and the Study of Torah', in Shemuel Safrai and Menahem Stern (eds), *The Jewish People in the First Century* (2 vols, CRINT 1.1–2; Assen: Van Gorcum; Philadelphia: Fortress, 1974–6), pp. 2:945–70; quotation from p. 952. Safrai ('Education and the Study of Torah', pp. 953–5) remarks further, depending on *y. Meg.* 3.1 (73d); *y. Ketub.* 13.1 (35c), that schools were connected with synagogues and that learning Torah was obligatory for boys but not for girls. But do these traditions really tell us anything about Jewish literacy in the first century?

26 On doubts about the rabbinic portait of widespread literacy Uncritical acceptance of the rabbinic tradition of schools in every village is rightly criticized in J. P. Meier, *A Marginal Jew: Rethinking the Historical Jesus, Vol. 1, The Roots of the Problem and the Person* (New York: Doubleday, 1991), p. 271; and Craffert and Botha, 'Why Jesus Could Walk on the Sea but He Could not Read and Write', pp. 24–5.

27 On the probability that Jesus was literate See Paul Foster, 'Educating Jesus: The Search for a Plausible Context', *JSHJ* 4 (2006), pp. 7–33.

28 On the meaning of Rabbi as title prior to 70 ce See Shaye J. D. Cohen, 'Epigraphical Rabbis', *JQR* 72 (1981–2), pp. 1–17.

29 On Jesus and rabbinic teaching See Rainer Riesner, *Jesus als Lehrer* (WUNT 2/7; Tübingen: Mohr Siebeck, 1981); Bruce D. Chilton and Craig A. Evans, 'Jesus and Israel's Scriptures', in Bruce D. Chilton and Craig A. Evans (eds), *Studying the Historical Jesus: Evaluations of the State of Current Research* (NTTS 19; Leiden: Brill, 1994), pp. 281–335, here 285–98.

30 On the questions Jesus put to his critics See John A. T. Robinson, 'Did Jesus have a Distinctive Use of Scripture?', in his *Twelve More New Testament Studies* (London: SCM Press, 1984, pp. 35–43). Robinson has called this distinctive feature Jesus' 'challenging use' of Scripture. He rightly regards this feature as deriving from Jesus himself and not the early Christian community. See also James D. G. Dunn, *Jesus Remembered* (Christianity in the Making 1; Grand Rapids: Eerdmans, 2003), p. 314.

31 For a helpful tabulation of Jesus' use of Scripture See Richard T. France, *Jesus and the Old Testament: His Application of Old Testament Passages to Himself and His Mission* (London: Tyndale, 1971), pp. 259–63.

32 On the 'canon' of Jesus and his contemporaries See Craig A. Evans, 'The Scriptures of Jesus and His Earliest Followers', in Lee M. McDonald and James A. Sanders (eds), *The Canon Debate* (Peabody, MA: Hendrickson, 2002), pp. 185–95.

33 On the 'canon' of Qumran In the non-biblical scrolls of Qumran and the region of the Dead Sea (here the *pesharim* are being excluded), the book of Deuteronomy is quoted some 22 times, Isaiah some 35 times and the Psalter some 31 times. See James C. VanderKam, 'Authoritative Literature in the Dead Sea Scrolls', *Dead Sea Discoveries* 5 (1998), pp. 382–402; 'Question of Canon Viewed through the Dead Sea Scrolls', in McDonald and Sanders (eds), *The Canon Debate*, pp. 91–109.

34 On rabbinic and scribal education: One is reminded of the rabbinic dictum: 'Scripture leads to Targum, Targum leads to Mishnah, Mishnah leads to Talmud, Talmud leads to performance' (*Sipre Deut.* §161 (on Deut. 17.19)). Although this dictum postdates Jesus by centuries, it probably in part mirrors earlier concepts of scribal pedagogy.

4 Confronting the establishment: ruling priests and the temple

1 ON THE MEANING OF ISAIAH 5 IN THE TIME OF JESUS See Joseph M. Baumgarten, '4Q500 and the Ancient Conception of the Lord's Vineyard', *JJS* 40 (1989), pp. 1–6; George J. Brooke, '4Q500 1 and the Use of Scripture in the Parable of the Vineyard', *DSD* 2 (1995), pp. 268–94.

2 ON THE TEMPLE WARNING INSCRIPTIONS See Charles S. Clermont-Ganneau, 'Une stèle du temple de Jérusalem', *RAr* 28 (1872), pp. 214–34, 290–6 + pl. X; Joseph M. Baumgarten, 'Exclusions from the Temple: Proselytes and Agrippa I', *JJS* 33 (1982), pp. 215–25; Peretz Segal, 'The Penalty of the Warning Inscription from the Temple of Jerusalem', *IEJ* 39 (1989), pp. 79–84.

3 ON DISPLAYING THE TEMPLE UTENSILS FOR PUBLIC VIEWING See Daniel R. Schwartz, 'Viewing the Holy Utensils', *NTS* 32 (1986), pp. 153–9. Schwartz believes the custom of publicly displaying the holy utensils, presupposed in the apocryphal story found in P. Oxy. 840, is probably historical.

4 ON THE *MIQVA'OT* (RITUAL IMMERSION POOLS) AT THE TEMPLE AND ELSEWHERE See Ronny Reich, 'Ritual Baths', in Eric M. Meyers (ed.), *The Oxford Encyclopedia of Archaeology in the Near East* (New York: Oxford University Press, 1997), pp. 4:430–1; '*Miqva'ot* at Khirbet Qumran and the Jerusalem Connection', in Lawrence H. Schiffman, Emanuel Tov and James C. VanderKam (eds), *The Dead Sea Scrolls: Fifty Years After Their Discovery* (Jerusalem: Israel Exploration Society, 2000), pp. 728–33.

5 ON THE HOUSES OF THE WEALTHY, INCLUDING RULING PRIESTS See Magen Broshi, 'Excavations in the House of Caiaphas, Mount Zion', in Yigael Yadin (ed.), *Jerusalem Revealed: Archaeology in the Holy City* (Jerusalem: Israel Exploration Society, 1974), pp. 57–60. For the suggestion that Annas and Caiaphas shared the same residence, see Arthur Rupprecht, 'The House of Annas–Caiaphas', *Archaeology in the Biblical World* 1 (1991), pp. 4–17; Shimon Gibson, *The Final Days of Jesus: The Archaeological Evidence* (New York: HarperOne, 2009), p. 82. For discussion of the stone vessels, see Shimon Gibson, 'Stone Vessels of the Early Roman Period from Jerusalem and Palestine: A Reassessment', in G. Claudio Bottini, Leah Di Segni and L. Daniel Chrupcala (eds), *One Land – Many Cultures: Archaeological Studies in Honour of Stanislao Loffreda OFM* (Jerusalem: Franciscan Printing Press, 2003), pp. 287–308.

6 ON THE FAMILY TOMB OF ANNAS See Leen and Kathleen Ritmeyer, 'Akeldama: Potter's Field or High Priest's Tomb?' *BAR* 20/6 (1994), pp. 22–35, 76, 78.

7 ON THE CAIAPHAS OSSUARY INSCRIPTIONS See Ronny Reich, 'Ossuary Inscriptions from the Caiaphas Tomb', *Jerusalem Perspective* 4/4–5 (1991), pp. 13–21 + plates and facsimiles; 'Ossuary Inscriptions from the "Caiaphas" Tomb', *'Atiqot* 21 (1992), pp. 72–7 + figs 5 and 6.

8 ON JEWISH OSSUARIES AND THE GREEK GOD CHARON See Rachel Hachlili and Ann Killebrew, 'Was the Coin-on-Eye Custom a Jewish Burial Practice in the Second Temple Period?' *BA* 46 (1983), pp. 147–53, esp. 148–9; Zvi Greenhut, 'The "Caiaphas" Tomb in North Talpiyot, Jerusalem', *'Atiqot* 21 (1992), pp. 63–71, esp. 70. On the custom and belief in afterlife, see David Bivin, 'A Sadducee Who Believed in an Afterlife?' *Jerusalem Perspective* 4/4–5 (1991), p. 7.

9 ON DEPICTIONS OF BOATS IN TOMBS See Benjamin Mazar, *Beth She'arim: Report on the Excavations During 1936–1940, vol. 1, Catacombs 1–4* (New Brunswick, NJ: Rutgers University Press, 1973), pl. XX (= Beth She'arim, Hall P, catacomb no. 1); see also Erwin R. Goodenough, *Jewish Symbols in the Greco-Roman Period, vol. 1, The Archaeological Evidence from Palestine* (Bollingen Series 37; New York: Pantheon Books, 1953), pp. 97–8 (cf. Goodenough, *Jewish Symbols in the Greco-Roman Period, vol. 3*, nos 67 and 77), for examples in Palestine; and Goodenough, *Jewish Symbols in the Greco-Roman Period, vol. 2*, p. 43 (cf. Goodenough, *Jewish Symbols in the Greco-Roman Period, vol. 3*, no. 836), for an example in Rome.

10 MORE ON AFTERLIFE BOATS Saul Liberman, 'Some Aspects of After Life in Early Rabbinic Literature', in S. Lieberman et al. (eds), *Harry Austryn Wolfson: Jubilee Volume on the Occasion of His Seventy-Fifth Birthday*, vol. 2 (Jerusalem: American Academy for Jewish Research, 1965), pp. 495–532, esp. 512–13.

11 YET MORE ON AFTERLIFE BOATS Mazar, *Beth She'arim*, p. 129.

12 FOR SCHOLARS CONVINCED OF THE CAIAPHAS IDENTIFICATION See John Dominic Crossan and Jonathan L. Reed, *Excavating Jesus: Beneath the Stones, Behind the Texts* (San Francisco: HarperCollins, 2001), p. 242. Archaeologists who agree with the identification include Zvi Greenhut, 'The Caiaphas Tomb in North Talpiyot, Jerusalem', and Ronny Reich, 'Ossuary Inscriptions of the Caiaphas Family from Jerusalem', in H. Geva (ed.), *Ancient Jerusalem Revealed* (Jerusalem: Israel Exploration Society, 1994), pp. 219–22 and 223–5 respectively.

13 FOR SCHOLARS NOT CONVINCED OF THE CAIAPHAS IDENTIFICATION See Emile Puech, 'A-t-on redécouvert le tombeau du grand-prêtre Caïphe?' *MdB* 80 (1993), pp. 42–7; William Horbury, 'The "Caiaphas" Ossuaries and Joseph Caiaphas', *PEQ* 126 (1994), pp. 32–48.

14 FOR DEBATE ABOUT THE QUALITY OF THE CAIAPHAS TOMB See Puech, 'A-t-on redécouvert le tombeau du grand-prêtre Caïphe?', pp. 45–6; Gibson, *The Final Days of Jesus*, p. 83.

15 ON VOCALIZING THE CAIAPHAS OSSUARY NAME See Horbury, 'The "Caiaphas" Ossuaries', p. 41: *yod* rather than *waw* 'seems less likely'; p. 46: an 'ambiguous vowel letter is more probably *waw* than *yodh*'; and Puech, 'A-t-on redécouvert le tombeau du grand-prêtre Caïphe?', p. 46, who suggests Qopha or Qupha.

16 ON THE THEOPHILUS OSSUARY INSCRIPTION See Dan Barag and David Flusser, 'The Ossuary of Yehohanah Granddaughter of the High Priest Theophilus', *IEJ* 36 (1986), pp. 39–44, here 39; Levi Yizhaq Rahmani, *A Catalogue of Jewish Ossuaries in the Collections of the State of Israel* (Jerusalem: The Israel Antiquities Authority, 1994), p. 259 no. 871.

17 ON THE BOETHOS OSSUARY INSCRIPTION See Eleazar Lipa Sukenik 'A Jewish Tomb Cave on the Slope of Mount Scopus', *Qovetz* 3 (1934), pp. 62–73 (Hebrew), here 67; Rahmani, *A Catalogue of Jewish Ossuaries*, pp. 85–6 no. 41.

18 ON THE COLLECTION OF TAXES IN FIRST-CENTURY JEWISH PALESTINE See K. C. Hanson and Douglas E. Oakman, *Palestine in the Time of Jesus: Social Structures and Social Conflicts* (Minneapolis: Fortress, 1998), pp. 99–129; Douglas E. Oakman, *Jesus and the Peasants* (Matrix: The Bible in Mediterranean Context 4; Eugene, OR: Cascade Books, 2007), pp. 280–97.

19 FOR LAGRANGE'S QORBAN DISCOVERIES See Marie-Joseph Lagrange, 'Epigraphie sémitique', *RB* 2 (1893), pp. 220–2.

20 ON THE QORBAN INSCRIPTION NEAR THE TEMPLE MOUNT WALL See Benjamin Mazar, 'The Excavations South and West of the Temple Mount in Jerusalem: The Herodian Period', *BA* 33 (1970), pp. 47–60, here 55 + fig. 13.

21 ON THE QORBAN OSSUARY INSCRIPTION See Józef Tadeusz Milik, 'Trois tombeaux juifs récemment découverts au Sud-Est de Jérusalem', *LÄ* 7 (1956–7), pp. 232–67, here 235–9 + figs 2 and 3; Joseph A. Fitzmyer, 'The Aramaic Qorbân Inscription from Jebel Hallet et-Tûrî and Mk 7:11/Mt 15:5', *JBL* 78 (1959), pp. 60–5.

22 ON THE DISCOVERY AND ANALYSIS OF THE CONTENTS OF THE SHROUD TOMB See Mark Spigelman, 'The Jerusalem Shroud: A Second Temple Burial Answers Modern Medical Questions', *Bulletin of the Anglo-Israel Archaeological Society* 24 (2006), p. 127; Gibson, *The Final Days of Jesus*, pp. 138–47.

23 ON THE MEDICAL EXAMINATION OF THE SKELETAL REMAINS OF THE CAIAPHAS TOMB See Joe Zias, 'Human Skeletal Remains from the "Caiaphas" Tomb', *'Atiqot* 21 (1992), pp. 78–80.

24 ON THE TOMB OF JASON See Levi Yizhaq Rahmani, 'Jason's Tomb', *IEJ* 17 (1967), pp. 61–100.

25 FOR A RECENT SURVEY OF THE EVIDENCE OF LONGEVITY IN JEWISH LATE ANTIQUITY See Yossi Nagar and Hagit Torgeë, 'Biological Characteristics of Jewish Burial in the Hellenistic and Early Roman Periods', *IEJ* 53 (2003), pp. 164–71.

5 Life with the dead: Jewish burial traditions

1 FOR INTRODUCTION TO JEWISH OSSILEGIUM See Eric M. Meyers, *Jewish Ossuaries: Reburial and Rebirth* (BibOr 24; Rome: Pontifical Biblical Institute, 1971); Craig A. Evans, *Jesus and the Ossuaries: What Jewish Burial Practices Reveal about the Beginning of Christianity* (Waco, TX: Baylor University Press, 2003); Byron R. McCane, *Roll Back the Stone: Death and Burial in the World of Jesus* (Harrisburg, PA: Trinity Press International, 2003).

2 FOR DETAILED DISCUSSION OF THE 'CRUCIFIXION' TEXTS FROM QUMRAN See Gregory L. Doudna, *4Q Pesher Nahum: A Critical Edition* (JSPSup 35; CIS 8; London and New York: Sheffield Academic Press, 2001), pp. 389–433; Yigael Yadin, *The Temple Scroll* (3 vols, Jerusalem: Israel Exploration Society, 1977–83), pp. 2:288–91.

3 FOR A SELECTION OF STUDIES CONCERNED WITH THIS FIND See Yigael Yadin, 'Epigraphy and Crucifixion', *IEJ* 23 (1973), pp. 18–22 + plate; Joe Zias and Eliezer Sekeles, 'The Crucified Man from Giv'at ha-Mivtar: A Reappraisal', *IEJ* 35 (1985), pp. 22–7; Joe Zias and James H. Charlesworth, 'Crucifixion: Archaeology, Jesus, and the Dead Sea Scrolls', in James H. Charlesworth (ed.), *Jesus and the Dead Sea Scrolls* (ABRL; New York: Doubleday, 1992), pp. 273–89 + plates. On the problem of determining bone damage before or after death, see Norman J. Sauer, 'The Timing of Injuries and Manner of Death: Distinguishing among Antemortem, Perimortem and Postmortem Trauma', in Kathleen J. Reichs (ed.), *Forensic Osteology: Advances in the Identification of Human Remains* (2nd edn, Springfield, IL: Charles C. Thomas, 1998), pp. 321–32.

4 FOR STUDIES RELATING TO THE DECAPITATED WOMAN (OR MAN) See N. Haas, 'Anthropological Observations on the Skeletal Remains from Giv'at ha-Mivtar', *IEJ* 20 (1970), pp. 38–59; Joe Zias, 'Anthropological Evidence of Interpersonal Violence in First-Century A.D. Jerusalem', *Current Anthropology* 24 (1983), pp. 233–4; Patricia Smith, 'The Human Skeletal Remains from the Abba Cave', *IEJ* 27 (1977), pp. 121–4.

5 On decapitation as act of violence and not judicial execution See Zias, 'Anthropological Evidence of Interpersonal Violence', pp. 123–4.

6 For assessment of the human remains at Towton V. Fiorato, A. Boylston and C. Knüsel (eds), *Blood Red Roses: The Archaeology of a Mass Grave from the Battle of Towton AD 1461* (Oxford: Oxbow, 2000).

7 For the argument that paucity of evidence for the burial of the executed implies Jesus was not buried See John Dominic Crossan, *Who Killed Jesus? Exposing the Roots of Anti-Semitism in the Gospel Story of the Death of Jesus* (San Francisco: HarperCollins, 1995), pp. 160–88.

8 On Roman burial practices See Jocelyn M. C. Toynbee, *Death and Burial in the Roman World* (Ithaca, NY: Cornell University Press, 1971).

9 On monumental tombs See Janos Fedak, *Monumental Tombs of the Hellenistic Age: A Study of Selected Tombs from the pre-Classical to the Early Imperial Era* (Toronto: University of Toronto Press, 1990); Geoffrey B. Waywell and Andrea Berlin, 'Monumental Tombs: From Maussollos to the Maccabees', *BAR* 33/3 (2007), pp. 54–65.

10 On the probability of the burial of Jesus See Raymond E. Brown, 'The Burial of Jesus (Mark 15:42–47)', *CBQ* 50 (1988), pp. 233–45.

11 On the element of shame in the burial of Jesus See Byron R. McCane, '"Where No One Had Yet Been Laid": The Shame of Jesus' Burial', in Bruce D. Chilton and Craig A. Evans (eds), *Authenticating the Activities of Jesus* (NTTS 28.2; Leiden: Brill, 1998), pp. 431–52; reprinted in McCane, *Roll Back the Stone*, pp. 89–108.

12 On the Gospels' consistency with archaeological evidence See Jodi Magness, 'Jesus' Tomb – What Did It Look Like?', in Hershel Shanks (ed.), *Where Christianity Was Born* (Washington, DC: Biblical Archaeology Society, 2008), pp. 213–26; quotation from p. 224. For criticism of Crossan's theory that Jesus was not buried, see McCane, *Roll Back the Stone*, p. 107, n. 6; Magness, 'Jesus' Tomb', pp. 222–4.

Appendix 1: Have we found the family tomb of Jesus?

1 For scholarly publications of the excavation of the East Talpiot tomb See Yosef Gat, 'East Talpiot', *Hadashot Arkheologiyot* [= *Archaeological News*] 76 (1981), pp. 24–5 (Hebrew); Amos Kloner,

'A Tomb with Inscribed Ossuaries in East Talpiyot, Jerusalem', *'Atiqot* 29 (1996), pp. 15–22 (with sketches by Shimon Gibson).

2 On the theory that the East Talpiot tomb belonged to the family of Jesus See Simcha Jacobovici and Charles Pellegrino, *The Jesus Family Tomb: The Discovery, the Investigation, and the Evidence that Could Change History* (San Francisco: HarperCollins, 2007). The release of this book coincided with a television documentary that aired on Discovery Channel and other cable outlets. Neither author is an archaeologist, historian or biblical scholar.

3 On the proper identification of the stonemason's mark in the 'Jesus' ossuary See Levi Yizhaq Rahmani, *A Catalogue of Jewish Ossuaries in the Collections of the State of Israel* (Jerusalem: The Israel Antiquities Authority, 1994), p. 223, n. 704. If one flips to pp. 226–9 one will see three more examples of ossuaries (nos 725, 729 and 731) from East Talpiot and a fourth from Ramot (no. 740) with X-marks. Perusal of Rahmani's catalogue will reveal many more examples of ossuaries bearing stonemason's marks. Jacobovici and Pellegrino reference Rahmani's catalogue. See *The Jesus Family Tomb*, p. 215. There is no defence for their misleading interpretation of this mark.

4 On the pointed gable and circle as a Christian symbol See Jacobovici and Pellegrino, *The Jesus Family Tomb*, pp. 11–12, 128–30. Jacobovici and Pellegrino refer to the pointed gable as a 'chevron' and as a 'secret Judeo-Christian symbol'. Nothing could be further from the truth.

5 On the pointed gable and circle or rosette in Jewish settings See Erwin R. Goodenough, *Jewish Symbols in the Greco-Roman Period*, vol. 3 (Bollingen Series 37; New York: Pantheon Books, 1953), figs 142 and 143, 239 (ossuaries), 508 (tomb facade); 676 (coin struck by Philip, tetrarch of Gaulanitis); 707 and 710 (epitaph art: Torah arks with gable and circle); for commentary on fig. 710, see Goodenough, *Jewish Symbols*, vol. 2: 'I should judge that the circle within the gable would have been a wreath or rosette in a larger drawing' (p. 6). See also Michael Avi-Yonah, *Art in Ancient Palestine: Selected Studies* (Jerusalem: Magnes Press, 1981), plates 12.4, 13.8, 15.4–5 and 16.1.

6 On the significance of Hasmonean names The Hasmonean family was an aristocratic priestly family that led the Jewish revolt against the Seleucid Greeks in 167 BCE. Their names became very popular among the Jewish people. Every name inscribed on the ossuaries in the East Talpiot tomb is Hasmonean. This coincidence, along with the prominent pointed gable and circle over the entrance to the tomb, suggests the occupants of the East Talpiot tomb were

affiliated with the Jerusalem temple and perhaps were members of the priestly aristocracy.

7 For a severely critical review of Jacobovici and Pellegrino, The Jesus Family Tomb See Shimon Gibson, *The Final Days of Jesus: The Archaeological Evidence* (New York: HarperOne, 2009), pp. 175–87: 'nothing to commend this tomb'; Jonathan Reed, in *Review of Biblical Literature* (posted online June 2007). Reed, a qualified and respected archaeologist, with justification speaks of 'deceit' in the Jacobovici/Pellegrino book. Even more egregious is the television documentary.

Appendix 2: What did Jesus look like?

1 Reconstructed Jesus face Produced by Richard Neave, retired medical artist, University of Manchester. See *Popular Mechanics* (7 December 2002).

2 For mummy portraits See Susan Walker and Morris Bierbrier (eds), *Ancient Faces: Mummy Portraits from Roman Egypt* (London: British Museum Press, 1997; 2nd edn, New York: Routledge, 2000); Jan Picton, Stephen Quirke and Paul C. Roberts (eds), *Living Images: Egyptian Funerary Portraits in the Petrie Museum* (Walnut Creek, CA: Left Coast Press, 2007); Alan K. and Michael Brady (eds), *Images and Artefacts of the Ancient World* (Oxford and New York: Oxford University Press, 2005), pp. 131–50.

3 What about the face of Jesus in the Shroud of Turin or on sixth- and seventh-century ce Byzantine coins? The image of the face in the Shroud of Turin and its resemblance to the face of Jesus stamped on Byzantine coins are interesting observations. But the science and authenticity of the Shroud are much disputed and the Byzantine coins are late. Reconstructing the face of Jesus on the basis of these items is not recommended.

4 On the clothing and textiles found at Nahal Hever See Y. Yadin, *Bar-Kokhba: The Rediscovery of the Legendary Hero of the Last Jewish Revolt against Imperial Rome* (London: Weidenfeld & Nicolson, 1971), pp. 66–85; Jodi Magness, *Debating Qumran: Collected Essays on its Archaeology* (Interdisciplinary Studies in Ancient Culture and Religion 4; Leuven: Peeters, 2004), pp. 113–49, esp. 137–40. Magness compares Yadin's finds with the textiles, shoes and clothing found at Qumran. For discussion of Roman clothing, with some comparison to Yadin's finds, see also Judith L. Sebesta, 'Tunica Ralla, Tunica Spissa: The Colors and Textiles of Roman Costume', and Lucille A. Roussin, 'Costume in Roman Palestine: Archaeological Remains and the Evidence from the Mishnah', in Judith L. Sebesta and Larissa Bonfante (eds), *The World of Roman*

Costume (Madison: University of Wisconsin Press, 2001), pp. 65–76, 182–90 respectively. Roussin's study correlates the archaeological evidence with the many comments about clothing in the rabbinic literature. She makes several interesting comments about how clothing reflected social status and religious traditions. In the same collection of studies, see also Douglas R. Edwards, 'The Social, Religious, and Political Aspects of Costume in Josephus', pp. 153–62.

5 ON JEWISH SANDALS AND OTHER LEATHER GOODS See Ann E. Killebrew, 'Leather Goods', in Lawrence H. Schiffman and James C. VanderKam (eds), *Encyclopedia of the Dead Sea Scrolls* (2 vols, Oxford: Oxford University Press, 2000), pp. 1:477–9.

6 ROMAN FOOTWEAR See Alan K. Bowman and J. David Thomas, *The Vindolanda Writing Tablets* (Newcastle-upon-Tyne: Frank Graham, 1974), p. 27 (pl. XIII). For technical discussion, see C. van Driel-Murray, 'Vindolanda and the Dating of Roman Footwear', *Britannia* 32 (2001), pp. 185–97. For general discussion, see N. Goldman, 'Roman Footwear', in Sebesta and Bonfante (eds), *The World of Roman Costume*, pp. 101–32.

Suggestions for further reading

We are fortunate in having a growing number of studies in archaeology. For those interested in further study of Jesus and archaeology, I recommend the following:

Books

Aviam, M., *Jews, Pagans and Christians in Galilee: 25 Years of Archaeological Excavations and Surveys. Hellenistic to Byzantine Periods* (Land of Galilee 1; Rochester, NY: University of Rochester Press, 2004).

Bagatti, B., *Excavations in Nazareth: Vol. 1, From the Beginning till the XII Century* (2 vols, Publications of the Studium Biblicum Franciscanum 17; Jerusalem: Franciscan Printing Press, 1969).

Bottini, G. C., Di Segni, L. and Alliata, E. (eds), *Christian Archaeology in the Holy Land, New Discoveries: Essays in Honour of Virgilio C. Corbo, OFM* (Studium Biblicum Franciscanum: Collectio Maior 36; Jerusalem: Franciscan Printing Press, 1990).

Charlesworth, J. H. (ed.), *Jesus and Archaeology* (Grand Rapids, MI: Eerdmans, 2006).

Charlesworth, J. H. and Weaver, W. P. (eds), *What Has Archaeology To Do with Faith?* (Faith and Scholarship Colloquies; Philadelphia, PA: Trinity Press International, 1992).

Crossan, J. D. and Reed, J. L., *Excavating Jesus: Beneath the Stones, Behind the Texts* (San Francisco, CA: HarperCollins, 2001).

Edwards, D. R. and McCollough, C. T. (eds), *Archaeology and the Galilee: Texts and Contexts in the Graeco-Roman and Byzantine Periods* (South Florida Studies in the History of Judaism 143; Atlanta, GA: Scholars Press, 1997).

Edwards, D. R. and McCollough, C. T. (eds), *The Archaeology of Difference: Gender, Ethnicity, Class and the 'Other' in Antiquity: Studies in Honor of Eric M. Meyers* (AASOR 60/61; Boston, MA: American Schools of Oriental Research, 2007).

Evans, C. A., *Jesus and the Ossuaries: What Jewish Burial Practices Reveal about the Beginning of Christianity* (Waco, TX: Baylor University Press, 2003).

Fant, C. and Reddish, M. G., *Lost Treasures of the Bible: Understanding the Bible through Archaeological Artifacts in World Museums* (Grand Rapids, MI: Eerdmans, 2008).

Gibson, S., *The Final Days of Jesus: The Archaeological Evidence* (New York: HarperOne, 2009).

Meyers, E. M. (ed.), *Galilee through the Centuries: Confluence of Cultures* (Duke Judaic Studies 1; Winona Lake, IN: Eisenbrauns, 1999).

Meyers, E. M. and Strange, J. F., *Archaeology, the Rabbis and Early Christianity* (London: SCM Press, 1981).

Murphy-O'Connor, J., *The Holy Land: An Oxford Archaeological Guide from Earliest Times to 1700* (5th edn, Oxford and New York: Oxford University Press, 2008).

Pixner, B., *Paths of the Messiah and Sites of the Early Church from Galilee to Jerusalem: Jesus and Jewish Christianity in Light of Archaeological Discoveries* (ed. R. Riesner; San Francisco, CA: Ignatius Press, 2010).

Reed, J., *Archaeology and the Galilean Jesus: A Re-examination of the Evidence* (Harrisburg, PA: Trinity Press International, 2000).

Runesson, A., Binder, D. D. and Olsson, B., *The Ancient Synagogue from its Origins to 200 CE: A Source Book* (Leiden: Brill, 2010).

Shanks, H. (ed.), *Where Christianity Was Born* (Washington, DC: Biblical Archaeology Society, 2006).

Sheler, Jeffrey L., *Is the Bible True? How Modern Debates and Discoveries Affirm the Essence of the Scriptures* (San Francisco, CA: HarperCollins, 1999).

Wachsmann, S., *The Sea of Galilee Boat: A 2000-Year-Old Discovery from the Sea of Legends* (Cambridge, MA: Perseus, 2000).

Waxman, S., *Loot: The Battle over the Stolen Treasures of the World* (New York: Henry Holt and Company, 2008).

Journals

American Journal of Archaeology
Ancient Near Eastern Studies
Archaeology
Archaeology in the Biblical World
Biblical Archaeologist
Biblical Archaeology Review
Bulletin of the American Schools of Oriental Research
International Journal of Nautical Archaeology
Israel Exploration Journal
Journal of Archaeological Science
Journal of Field Archaeology
Journal of Marine Archaeology and Technology
Journal of Maritime Archaeology

Journal of Near Eastern Studies
Near Eastern Archaeology
Oxford Journal of Archaeology
Palestine Exploration Quarterly

Reference works

Fagan, B. M. (ed.), *The Oxford Companion to Archaeology* (Oxford and London: Oxford University Press, 1996).

Hicks, D. and Beaudry, M. C. (eds), *The Cambridge Companion to Historical Archaeology* (Cambridge: Cambridge University Press, 2006).

Meyers, E. M. (ed.), *The Oxford Encyclopedia of Archaeology in the Near East* (5 vols, New York: Oxford University Press, 1997).

Negev, A. and Gibson, S. (eds), *Archaeological Encyclopedia of the Holy Land* (rev. edn, New York: Continuum, 2001).

Stern, E. (ed.), *The New Encyclopedia of Archaeological Excavations in the Holy Land* (4 vols, Jerusalem: The Israel Exploration Society, 1993).

Stern, E. (ed.), *The New Encyclopedia of Archaeological Excavations in the Holy Land 5: Supplementary Volume* (Jerusalem: The Israel Exploration Society, 2008).

Index of ancient writings and sources

Index of modern names

185

Index of subjects

1 Clement 8
1 Corinthians 6
4Q246 3
4Q521 3
11QTemple 120

Aaron 17
Abraham 117–18
Accelerator Mass
    Spectrometry 12, 110
Acts 38, 43, 45, 80, 88, 98
Aelius Brocchus 68
Agrippa I 9, 98, 113, 129
Agrippa II 9, 96, 113
Akeldama 97, 110–11
Albinus 123
Alexamenos 73
Alexander (ruling priest)
    97
Alexander the Great 65
Alexandria 65, 74
alms/almsgiving 29
Amos, book of 87
Ananel (high priest) 101
Ananias (early Christian)
    115
Ananias (high priest)
    101–3, 105
Anaxilaus 18
Andrew 7
Annas 9, 96–7, 99, 101–2,
    133, 167 n. 5
Annius Rufus 123
Annunciation 3
Antigonus 51
Antioch 8
Antiochus I Soter 51
Antiochus IV Epiphanes
    22, 39, 57, 74
Antipas 9, 15, 28, 32, 45
Antipater (the Cynic) 17
Antoninus Pius 26
'Aqavia 102–3

Aramaic 21
Aristobulus (high priest)
    101
Ashmolean Museum xi
Asia Minor 7–8, 65
Astylus and Pardalus,
    Bar of 70
Athens 65
Augustine 83
Augustus 58, 73, 120
Autographs 76

Bar Kokhba 43, 58
Bar Kokhba Caves 151
basalt 31, 46–49
Batavians, ninth cohort of
    68
BBC 142
beheading 125–26
Beinicke Rare Book and
    Manuscript Library xi
Belial 35
Benjamin (patriarch) 118
Berenice 96
Berenike 41
Beth Shearim 147
Bethlehem 13, 144
Bodleian Library xi
Boethos 104–5
British Museum xi, 133
burial 11, 113–40, 144
Burnt House 103, 107

Caesar 26, 39, 138
Caesarea Maritima 13–14,
    30, 122
Caesarea Philippi 30
Caiaphas 9, 94, 96–102,
    111, 141, 147, 167 n. 5
Cairo *Damascus
    Document* 29
Caligula 120
Calliope 68–9

Canaan 118
canon 87
Cantheras 104
Capernaum 13, 21, 31–2,
    36, 45–9, 64
Capitoline triad 26
carbon dating 12
CAT scan 12, 70
*Catalogue of Jewish
    Ossuaries* 146
Cave of Letters 151
Celsus Library 65
Cephas *see* Peter
Charon 98–9
Chester Beatty Papyri 76
Chorazin 60–1
Chronicles, books of 87
Church of the
    Annunciation 14
Claudia Severa 68–9
Claudius 120
Clement of Rome 8–9
Cleopatra 65
clothing 148–52,
    173 nn. 4–5
Codex Ephraemi
    Rescriptus 165 n. 23
Codex Sinaiticus 165 n. 23
Codex Vaticanus 75
coins 26, 51, 97, 134,
    173 n. 3
Collegio Romano 71
colobium 71
Coponius 123
Corinth 7–8, 65
Cornelius 79
Crates 17
criminals 116–17, 120,
    126–30, 137
cross, crucifixion 6, 9,
    120–30, 137, 145
crurifragium 124–5
Cuspius Pansa, House of 70

188